Titanic

The Shocking Secrets Buried
Beneath the Waves

*(The History and Legacy of the World's Most
Famous Ship)*

Jeff Glenn

Published By **Frank Joseph**

Jeff Glenn

All Rights Reserved

Titanic: The Shocking Secrets Buried Beneath the Waves (The History and Legacy of the World's Most Famous Ship)

ISBN 978-1-7781462-3-7

No part of this guidebook shall be reproduced in any form without permission in writing from the publisher except in the case of brief quotations embodied in critical articles or reviews.

Legal & Disclaimer

The information contained in this book is not designed to replace or take the place of any form of medicine or professional medical advice. The information in this book has been provided for educational & entertainment purposes only.

The information contained in this book has been compiled from sources deemed reliable, and it is accurate to the best of the Author's knowledge; however, the Author cannot guarantee its accuracy and validity and cannot be held liable for any errors or omissions. Changes are periodically made to this book. You must consult your doctor or get professional medical advice before using any of the suggested remedies, techniques, or information in this book.

Upon using the information contained in this book, you agree to hold harmless the Author from and against any damages, costs, and expenses, including any legal fees potentially resulting from the application of any of the information provided by this guide. This disclaimer applies to any damages or injury caused by the use and application, whether directly or indirectly, of any advice or information presented, whether for breach of contract, tort, negligence, personal injury, criminal intent, or under any other cause of action.

You agree to accept all risks of using the information presented inside this book. You need to consult a professional medical practitioner in order to ensure you are both able and healthy enough to participate in this program.

Table Of Contents

Chapter 1: The Maiden Voyage 1

Chapter 2: A Melting Pot Of Stories 10

Chapter 3: Life Aboard The Titanic 20

Chapter 4: The Fatal Encounter 29

Chapter 5: Sos And Rescue Efforts 39

Chapter 6: Investigations And Inquiries .. 49

Chapter 7: Titanic In Popular Culture 59

Chapter 8: Memorials And Memorabilia. 65

Chapter 9: The Olympic And Britannic 74

Chapter 10: A Timeless Legend 81

Chapter 11: A Symbol Of Human Hubris And Resilience 85

Chapter 12: The Unsinkable Ship Myths And Realities 92

Chapter 13: The Passengers Aboard Titanic 99

Chapter 14: The Night The Titanic Sank 109

Chapter 15: The Search For Titanic 121

Chapter 16: Titanic's Enduring Mysteries 132

Chapter 17: Birth Of The Legend 142

Chapter 18: Design And Construction ... 159

Chapter 19: Maiden Voyage 174

Chapter 1: The Maiden Voyage

Setting the Stage: Early twentieth Century Travel and the Age of Luxury

In the early 20th century, the sector professional a revolution in journey and transportation Steamships had turn out to be the dominant mode of long-distance adventure, connecting a long way flung continents and ushering in a current generation of global connectivity. As an brand of this technological development and luxury, the White Star Line, one of the primary transport companies of the time, released into an bold challenge to collect the grandest and most high priced passenger liner ever conceived—the RMS Titanic.

The Birth of the Titanic: An Ambitious Project

The idea of building the Titanic and its sister ships, Olympic and Britannic, originated from the vision of the White Star Line's chairman, J. Bruce Ismay, and the American financier J.P. Morgan. They sought to outdo their opposition, the Cunard Line, in developing the most crucial and most opulent vessels ever seen at the seas. The deliver's format have become assigned to Thomas Andrews, the handling director of Harland and Wolff shipyard in Belfast, Northern Ireland, one of the maximum prominent shipbuilders of the time.

The creation of the Titanic began out out on March 31, 1909, with a grand rite marking the laying of the keel—the deliver's basis. Over the following years, thousands of expert human beings toiled tirelessly to convey the vessel to life. From its huge hull to the trendy interior, every element modified into cautiously deliberate and performed.

Preparations for the Inaugural Voyage

On May 31, 1911, after sizeable manufacturing and outfitting, the Titanic grow to be prepared for its first sea trials. The trials have been accomplished to ensure the deliver's seaworthiness, checking out its engines, steering, and navigation structures.

Satisfied with the effects, the shipbuilders and the White Star Line prepared for the Titanic's maiden voyage, which changed into scheduled for April 10, 1912.

The anticipation and pleasure surrounding the Titanic's maiden voyage have been exceptional. The media covered every element of the ship's centers, heralding it as the pinnacle of pricey and comfort. Prominent human beings from diverse walks of lifestyles, together with millionaires, politicians, artists, and immigrants searching for a new existence in America, eagerly booked passage in this historic adventure.

As the Titanic organized to set sail from Southampton, England, to New York City, USA, the surroundings modified into taken into consideration one in every of glamour and birthday party. The deliver's departure might be the start of a momentous and unforgettable journey throughout the Atlantic—a journey that could in the long run seal the Titanic's vicinity in records.

Little did absolutely everyone apprehend that destiny had one-of-a-type plans, and the Titanic's maiden voyage need to cause tragedy, leaving an indelible mark on the annals of maritime history. The Titanic's story may additionally want to circulate right now to be a effective reminder of the human spirit's resilience, in addition to a cautionary tale about the effects of overconfidence within the face of nature's may probably. In the subsequent chapters, we're capable of delve deeper into the events that induced the Titanic's sinking, the memories of the passengers and organization, the aftermath, and the iconic legacy of this unsinkable legend.

Building the Titanic: A Dream and its Realization

Construction Challenges and Innovations

Building the Titanic changed into a huge venture that presented numerous demanding situations to the designers, engineers, and people worried. The supply's sheer length, coupled with the choice for opulence and innovation, pushed the limits of shipbuilding technology on the time.

One of the primary challenges grow to be the enormous scale of the vessel. The Titanic measured about 882 toes lengthy and stood over a hundred 75 toes tall from keel to the pinnacle of its funnels. Its large size required advanced engineering strategies to make sure structural integrity. To guide its weight and save you sagging, the Titanic featured 15 watertight bulkheads, which have been presupposed to make the supply certainly unsinkable.

In phrases of propulsion, the Titanic utilized a combination of reciprocating steam engines and turbine engines. This hybrid propulsion gadget modified into speculated to offer every energy and gasoline standard overall performance. The supply should acquire a most pace of round 23 knots (26.Five mph), a great feat for a vessel of its period and time.

Launching and Outfitting the Titanic

The Titanic's production occurred on the Harland and Wolff shipyard in Belfast, Northern Ireland. After nearly three years of tough paintings, the supply become geared up to be launched into the water. On May 31, 1911, a crowd of spectators gathered to witness this momentous occasion. To help with the discharge, 22 heaps of tallow and cleaning cleaning soap were unfold alongside the slipway to lubricate the deliver's direction into the River Lagan.

At precisely 12:15 PM, the Titanic commenced out its sluggish descent down the slipway. As it entered the water, the hull displacement because of the supply's weight created waves that damaged close by ships and washed away some spectators' belongings. Nevertheless, the discharge changed into a fulfillment, and the deliver modified into moved to a becoming-out berth for the very last diploma of advent.

Over the following numerous months, the indoors of the Titanic turn out to be converted right right into a floating palace. The supply featured lavish services, which incorporates a super ingesting saloon decorated with pricey woodwork, a grand staircase, a swimming pool, a gymnasium, a squash courtroom docket, and a Turkish tub. The quality cabins had been elegantly furnished, with a few boasting private promenade decks.

The 2nd-beauty and 1/3-elegance resorts, whilst not as extravagant because the first-rate areas, had been still cushty and provided greater services than maximum passengers had ever skilled earlier than.

The White Star Line and Its Vision

The White Star Line, installation in 1845, grow to be a British transport enterprise appeared for its hobby on passenger consolation and safety. It competed fiercely with outstanding shipping traces, maximum substantially the Cunard Line, in the beneficial transatlantic passenger change.

The Titanic, collectively with its sister ships Olympic and Britannic, turn out to be designed to be the pinnacle of luxury tour on the North Atlantic path. The White Star Line marketed its new trio because the maximum stable and maximum steeply-priced ships afloat, seeking out to attract rich and discerning vacationers who sought the last experience in transatlantic crossings.

The White Star Line's imaginative and prescient for the Titanic end up now not pretty a incredible deal developing a income however moreover about retaining British dominance inside the maritime worldwide. The deliver represented the epitome of British engineering and design, presupposed to exhibit the u . S . A .'s naval prowess and technological achievements.

However, the pursuit of high-priced and opulence, coupled with a focal point on tempo and duration, inadvertently contributed to the Titanic's vulnerability. Despite the ship's watertight bulkheads, inadequate policies, and the lack of enough lifeboats, it modified into believed that the Titanic modified into almost unsinkable—a notion that is probably tragically disproven on its maiden voyage.

In the following chapters, we're able to explore the events important as an awful lot because the Titanic's fateful come upon with an iceberg, the human memories on board, the aftermath of the disaster, and the some distance-conducting effect that the sinking of the "unsinkable" ship had on maritime records and global reputation.

Chapter 2: A Melting Pot Of Stories

The Titanic's passenger list turn out to be a contemplated image of the social and economic sort of early 20th-century transatlantic tour. From the elite and extraordinary people in first-rate to the center-class passengers in 2d-magnificence and the hopeful immigrants searching out a state-of-the-art lifestyles in 1/three-elegance, every agency had their own particular testimonies and dreams. Alongside the passengers, the institution human beings performed a important function in ensuring the easy operation of the deliver. Let us delve into the lives and reviews of those numerous organizations onboard the Titanic.

Section 1: First-Class: The Elite and Prominent

The extremely good passengers at the Titanic represented a number of the wealthiest and most influential people of their time. Among them were industrialists, business tycoons, celebrities, and aristocrats trying to find the great and most high-priced tour revel in to be had. The hotels for fine passengers have been extraordinary, featuring lavish suites, personal prom decks, and costly lounges.

Notable brilliant passengers included Benjamin Guggenheim, an American mining rich person; John Jacob Astor IV, a awesome businessman and real belongings developer; and Molly Brown, moreover called "The Unsinkable Molly Brown," an American socialite and philanthropist. Their recollections and moves subsequently of the sinking might emerge as mythical and characterize the braveness and resilience of those on board.

Section 2: Second-Class: The Middle Class Aboard

Second-class passengers have been predominantly composed of properly-to-do professionals, teachers, and tourists. While they did not enjoy the identical extravagant luxuries as those in great, their accommodations have been still cushty and provided get admission to to severa onboard facilities.

Second-elegance passengers have been frequently greater reserved approximately their backgrounds and social fame than the ones in amazing. They included humans like Lawrence Beesley, a trainer and creator who later wrote about his stories at the Titanic, and Elizabeth Catherine Walton Allen, a survivor who stored an intensive diary of her time at the supply.

Section three: Third-Class: Immigrants Seeking a New Life

The majority of passengers at the Titanic belonged to the 1/three-elegance, additionally referred to as "guidance." These passengers have been commonly immigrants looking for a better existence in America. They got here from various nations, which encompass Ireland, England, Scandinavia, the Middle East, and Eastern Europe.

For some of the 1/3-magnificence passengers, the Titanic represented an opportunity for a sparkling begin in a modern-day day land. The situations in 0.33-beauty were simple, with shared centers and dormitory-style snoozing preparations. Despite the modest hotels, the environment in 1/three-magnificence changed into regularly lively and colourful, as passengers bonded over their shared hopes and dreams.

Section 4: Crew Members: Essential Cogs inside the Ship's Machinery

Behind the scenes, the Titanic's group individuals worked tirelessly to make sure the clean operation of the ship. They got here from one-of-a-kind backgrounds and nationalities, taking walks in severa roles including engineers, stewards, chefs, wi-fi operators, and deckhands.

Among the crew had been the professional engineers and stokers who operated the deliver's engines, ensuring the Titanic's propulsion. The stewards and maids attended to the wishes of the passengers, retaining cleanliness and providing impeccable service.

The ship's wireless operators, Jack Phillips and Harold Bride, carried out a essential feature in communications. They have been accountable for sending and receiving messages, in conjunction with the misery calls even as the Titanic struck the iceberg.

The crew members confronted huge challenges sooner or later of the evacuation, as they labored tirelessly to make sure the passengers' safety and assist in the launching of lifeboats.

As we maintain to find out the Titanic's adventure, we're able to delve deeper into the man or woman tales of the passengers and team people, highlighting their moments of bravery, sacrifice, and humanity in the face of one of the most tragic maritime failures in statistics.

Departure from Southampton: The Voyage Begins

The Titanic's departure from Southampton on April 10, 1912, have end up a grand spectacle, attracting crowds of onlookers who accumulated to witness the departure of this majestic supply on its maiden voyage. The surroundings modified into one in every of pride and anticipation, as passengers and crew alike released into what become supposed to be a momentous and high-priced adventure in some unspecified time in the future of the Atlantic.

Farewell to Southampton:

At noon on April 10, 1912, the Titanic cast off its moorings and started its journey from the White Star Line's berth in Southampton, England. With the sound of cheering crowds echoing within the air, the supply majestically glided faraway from the dock, making its manner down the River Test and in the direction of the English Channel.

As the Titanic sailed away, its big length and sumptuous appearance left an prolonged-lasting affect at the onlookers, who waved farewell to pals, circle of relatives, and loved ones onboard. Little did they understand that this would be the last time they'll see many of the passengers and organization alive.

Cherbourg, France - First Stop:

After leaving Southampton, the Titanic's first port of name changed into Cherbourg, France. The supply arrived at Cherbourg later that middle of the night, wherein it modified into scheduled to pick out up greater passengers. A mild boat transported passengers from the shore to the Titanic, due to the reality the supply become too large to dock without delay at the port.

Queenstown (now Cobh), Ireland - Second Stop: The Titanic's final save you in advance than its transatlantic crossing became Queenstown (now Cobh), Ireland. On April 11, 1912, the Titanic arrived at Queenstown, wherein it anchored in the harbor. Here, extra passengers boarded the deliver, at the side of a set of Irish immigrants in search of a cutting-edge life in America.

Life Aboard During the Initial Days

As the Titanic made its manner throughout the Atlantic, lifestyles onboard in a few unspecified time within the destiny of the initial days changed into filled with a feel of pride and exploration. Passengers explored the supply's costly facilities, cherished the numerous onboard sports activities activities, and marveled on the technological wonders of the "unsinkable" vessel.

First-Class Luxury:

First-beauty passengers reveled within the lap of pricey for the duration of their journey. They enjoyed sumptuous food inside the grand consuming saloon, attended elegant soirées within the deliver's lounges, and strolled along the opulent promenade decks. Each day brought loads of sports and social gatherings, permitting passengers to indulge within the best studies available at sea.

Middle-Class Comforts:

Second-elegance passengers furthermore had get right of access to to more than a few offerings, although not as extravagant as the ones in first rate. They dined in a spacious eating room, loved enjoyment sports activities within the library and smoking room, and mingled with fellow passengers within the snug communal areas.

Third-Class Challenges and Community:

For 1/three-splendor passengers, lifestyles aboard the Titanic supplied its very personal set of stressful conditions. Their motels have been more easy, and shared facilities have been common. However, the spirit of camaraderie and the shared choice for a higher life in America fostered a strong experience of network among the ones passengers.

Crew Duties and Routines:

Meanwhile, the group individuals worked around the clock to ensure the deliver's clean operation and the comfort of the passengers.

From the engine room to the eating saloons, each institution member carried out a important role in keeping the Titanic going for walks efficiently.

As the Titanic sailed into the notable expanse of the Atlantic, passengers and group settled into their workouts, blind to the upcoming tragedy that would soon unfold. The ship's high-priced environment and the promise of a contemporary day starting in America filled the air, growing an air of thriller of optimism and pride for the adventure in advance.

In the subsequent chapters, we will discover the fateful occasions that brought about the Titanic's tragic encounter with an iceberg, the chaos and heroism at some level within the evacuation, the aftermath of the catastrophe, and the lasting effect that the sinking of this "unsinkable" deliver had on maritime statistics and the world.

Chapter 3: Life Aboard The Titanic

The notable inns aboard the Titanic have been now not anything short of opulent and extravagant, designed to cater to the maximum discerning and wealthy passengers of the early 20th century. These high priced regions rivaled the greatest lodges and homes of the time, presenting a degree of consolation and beauty that became amazing in maritime tour.

Staterooms and Suites:

First-magnificence passengers cherished non-public staterooms and suites, plenty of which have been fairly furnished and prepared with current centers. These lavish quarters featured cushty beds, high priced linens, and elegant furniture, imparting a flavor of home whilst at sea.

Grand Dining Saloon:

The grand eating saloon turn out to be the center piece of remarkable social lifestyles on the Titanic. It changed into an huge and ornate dining room that spanned the width of the deliver. Here, passengers were dealt with to gourmet food prepared via a set of expert chefs, served via attentive waitstaff.

A La Carte Restaurant:

In addition to the grand ingesting saloon, excellent passengers ought to dine at the à l. A. Carte eating place, offering a greater intimate and personalized consuming enjoy. The menu featured a huge shape of delicacies to healthy numerous tastes.

Lounges and Smoking Rooms:

First-class lounges were elegant areas where passengers have to lighten up, socialize, and revel in immoderate tea or cocktails. Some lounges featured grand pianos, top notch art work, and luxurious furnishings. There had been moreover precise smoking rooms for people who needed to take pleasure in tobacco.

Promenade Decks:

First-class passengers had high-quality get entry to to spacious promenade decks that wrapped across the deliver's outdoor. These decks supplied stunning perspectives of the sea and supplied a serene setting for leisurely strolls or non-public conversations.

Second and Third-Class Living Conditions

While not as extravagant as first rate, the second one and 0.33-splendor accommodations at the Titanic had been nevertheless taken into consideration quite comfortable for the time. These regions furnished passengers with critical amenities and communal spaces for socializing and rest.

Second-Class Cabins:

Second-beauty passengers had properly-appointed cabins that supplied a comfortable location to relaxation in a few unspecified time within the destiny in their journey. While the cabins had been smaller and lots less ornate than first-rate motels, they supplied a comfortable and alluring region for passengers.

Third-Class Berths and Dormitories:

Third-splendor passengers shared open berths and dormitory-fashion motels. These regions were extra number one and utilitarian in assessment to the non-public staterooms of brilliant. However, the 1/3-magnificence regions had been stored clean and cushty to ensure a pleasing adventure for all passengers.

Dining Facilities:

The second-splendor consuming room changed into spacious and furnished table issuer for meals. While the second-elegance menu was now not as big as first-rate, it although furnished quite a few tasty alternatives. Third-elegance passengers dined in large communal areas, and their meals have been organized in massive-scale kitchens.

Onboard Activities and Entertainment

The Titanic supplied a massive selection of activities and amusement to keep passengers engaged and entertained in the course of the adventure.

Live Music and Concerts:

Musicians and bands aboard the Titanic carried out numerous genres of tune, together with classical, popular tunes, and dance tune. The deliver's grand staircase modified into a famous spot for performances, and passengers should revel in live live performance events in the lounges and specific public areas.

Gymnasium and Sports:

The deliver boasted a very ready gym, allowing passengers to maintain their fitness physical activities on the equal time as at sea. There have been moreover deck video games and sports activities like shuffleboard for passengers to experience inside the sparkling sea air.

Reading and Writing Rooms:

For the ones looking for quiet moments, the Titanic presented reading and writing rooms stocked with books, newspapers, and stationery, providing a peaceful retreat for contemplation and meditated photo.

Smoking and Social Spaces:

The supply featured actual smoking rooms and social regions wherein passengers may additionally need to build up for verbal exchange, card video games, or without a doubt to experience the business enterprise of fellow vacationers.

Religious Services:

Religious offerings have been done at the Titanic, catering to the diverse ideals and faiths of the passengers. These services have been held in various languages to deal with particular nationalities on board.

Overall, the Titanic furnished a number of services and enjoyment options to make certain that passengers of all instructions had a snug and fun journey for the duration of the

Atlantic. Unfortunately, the birthday celebration of luxurious and modernity onboard may quick be overshadowed through the unthinkable events that lay earlier. In the following chapters, we are capable of explore the fateful night time time of April 14, 1912, even as the Titanic collided with an iceberg, the following chaos and heroic efforts to keep lives, and the long-lasting legacy of this tragic maritime disaster.

The Wonders of the Ship: Technological Marvels

The Titanic have become a wonder of engineering for its time, boasting severa technological upgrades that have been supposed to make it the maximum steady and maximum pricey deliver afloat. From its huge duration to its modern day protection abilties, the Titanic represented the pinnacle of early twentieth-century maritime generation.

The Titanic's Engineering Feats:

a. Double-Bottomed Hull: The Titanic's hull modified into constructed with a double-bottom design, which provided an added layer of safety within the path of functionality hull breaches. This layout have become speculated to lessen the risk of water ingress in case of a collision with an iceberg or unique items.

b. Watertight Bulkheads: The ship's hull became divided into 16 watertight booths with the aid of 15 transverse bulkheads. These bulkheads extended from the bottom of the supply as lots as B Deck. In the event of flooding, the watertight cubicles have been speculated to consist of the water and save you it from spreading at a few stage inside the deliver.

c. Riveting and Construction: The Titanic's hull modified into assembled the use of about three million rivets, which held the metallic plates together. The shipbuilders used contemporary-day hydraulic riveting machines to make sure a constant and watertight introduction.

d. Advanced Propulsion: The Titanic have become powered through the usage of a combination of reciprocating steam engines and turbine engines, offering the supply with wonderful tempo and performance for its period. The deliver's huge propellers have been powered via using 29 boilers, which burned coal to generate steam.

Radio Communications: The Role of Wireless Operators The Titanic's wi-fi telegraphy tool turn out to be considered one of its most crucial verbal exchange system and achieved a considerable function within the sports activities that spread out on that fateful night time.

Chapter 4: The Fatal Encounter

The Events Leading Up to the Tragedy

As the Titanic released into its maiden voyage from Southampton to New York City, severa factors and alternatives contributed to the disaster that could unfold at the night of April 14, 1912.

Ice Warnings: Throughout April 14, 1912, the Titanic acquired severa warnings of ice within the area. These warnings came from amazing ships in the place, at the side of the Californian, the Baltic, and the Mesaba. The wi-fi operators relayed these messages to the bridge, but they were now not taken as seriously as they need to have been.

High Speed: The Titanic end up crusing at a tempo of approximately 22 knots (about 25 mph) at the night time of the collision. Captain Edward J. Smith and others favored to gather New York earlier of time desk to make headlines and show off the ship's top notch tempo.

Lack of Binoculars: The lookouts within the crow's nest, Frederick Fleet and Reginald Lee, did now not have get entry to to binoculars, that would have potentially helped them spot the iceberg in advance.

Reduced Visibility: The night time of April 14 was pretty calm and easy, primary to a loss of visible waves breaking toward the bottom of the iceberg, making it more difficult for the lookouts to locate the chance.

The Fatal Night: April 14, 1912

On the night of April 14, 1912, the Titanic modified into crusing thru the North Atlantic, approximately four hundred miles south of Newfoundland, Canada. The environment onboard modified into one in every of party and pleasure, with passengers and institution playing the steeply-priced services of the deliver.

The Collision:

At 11:40 PM, while many passengers had been asleep or engaged in sports onboard, the Titanic struck an iceberg on its starboard (proper) aspect. The iceberg, which turn out to be noticed too beyond due to keep away from a collision, tore a chain of big gashes within the supply's hull below the waterline. The harm affected numerous of the deliver's watertight booths.

Response and Realization:

After the collision, the team quick realized the severity of the scenario. Captain Smith end up knowledgeable of the incident, and orders have been given to shut the watertight doors and prepare the lifeboats for a capability evacuation.

Distress Signals:

Wireless operators Jack Phillips and Harold Bride sent out distress signs using the CQD and SOS codes, alerting nearby ships of the Titanic's dire situation. The nearby passenger deliver RMS Carpathia, beneath the command of Captain Arthur Rostron, responded to the misery signs and started steaming inside the path of the Titanic's location.

The Collision: Eyewitness Accounts

Numerous eyewitness payments from passengers and organization members paint a shiny photo of the chaos and confusion that determined the collision.

Passengers' Accounts:

Many passengers stated feeling a mild shudder or vibration at the identical time as the ship struck the iceberg, but a few to begin with believed it modified into not anything critical. As the situation opened up, panic and confusion unfold the various passengers, who have been unsure of the quantity of the damage and the ability threat.

Crew Members' Actions:

The crew worked diligently to decrease the lifeboats and guide passengers to protection. The scarcity of lifeboats and absence of lifeboat drills delivered on a few confusion and delays in the path of the evacuation system.

Heroic Efforts:

Amidst the chaos, acts of heroism and selflessness emerged. Crew members and a few passengers displayed exquisite bravery and helped others into lifeboats, even on the threat of their non-public lives.

As the night time time wore on, it have come to be easy that the Titanic turn out to be swiftly sinking. The order changed into given for "girls and kids first" to board the lifeboats. The Carpathia arrived at the scene at round 4:00 AM, rescuing the survivors from the lifeboats and the icy waters. Tragically, over 1,500 passengers and crew misplaced their lives in one of the most infamous maritime screw ups in records.

In the following chapters, we are able to discover the recollections of the survivors, the heroic efforts of human beings at some stage in the evacuation, the inquiries and investigations that discovered the catastrophe, and the lasting effect of the Titanic's sinking on maritime protection rules and practices.

Chaos and Panic: Abandon Ship!

The Order to Abandon Ship: Saving Lives

After the Titanic struck the iceberg and the severity of the scenario became apparent, the order to barren region supply become given by way of the usage of Captain Edward J. Smith at round 12:15 AM on April 15, 1912. This critical order initiated the evacuation method, as institution contributors and passengers alike scrambled to get to the lifeboats and break out the sinking supply.

Women and Children First:

In accordance with the maritime manner of lifestyles of "women and youngsters first," priority end up given to ladies and kids to board the lifeboats. The idea changed into to make certain the safety of the maximum susceptible passengers in advance than permitting men to board the lifeboats.

Evacuation Challenges:

The Titanic have turn out to be designed to hold a whole of sixty 4 lifeboats, however it handiest had 20 lifeboats and four collapsible boats onboard. These lifeboats may also additionally need to deal with round 1,178 human beings, an extended way fewer than the whole capability of the deliver, that have grow to be over 3,500 passengers and crew. This shortage of lifeboats provided a fantastic task during the evacuation.

Lowering the Lifeboats:

Lowering the lifeboats was a tough mission, because of the fact the team had to navigate the lifeboats down the edges of the supply whilst it come to be listing (tilting) due to the flooding. Some lifeboats have been no longer crammed to their ability due to fears that they is probably damaged if completely loaded or problems about the supply's balance.

Lifeboats and Evacuation Challenges

The evacuation of the Titanic furnished numerous demanding situations that hindered the timely and inexperienced evacuation of all passengers and group.

Lack of Lifeboat Drills:

One crucial assignment modified into the shortage of entire lifeboat drills in some unspecified time in the future of the voyage. As a stop result, many passengers and crew members have been unexpected with the lifeboat launching strategies and had no longer been as it should be prepared for an emergency evacuation.

Language Barriers:

The Titanic carried passengers from one of a type nationalities, and not all organization contributors spoke the equal languages because the passengers. This language barrier occasionally triggered confusion in a few unspecified time in the future of the evacuation gadget, making it tough to offer easy commands to all passengers.

Initial Disbelief and Complacency:

Some passengers and group to start with did now not take transport of as genuine with that the supply end up in immoderate danger after the collision. The "unsinkable" popularity of the Titanic and the perception in the supply's advanced safety functions may moreover have brought approximately a experience of complacency, delaying the preliminary response to the emergency.

Heroism and Sacrifice: Bravery Amidst Disaster

Despite the demanding situations and chaos, numerous acts of heroism and sacrifice emerged at a few stage in the evacuation of the Titanic.

Crew Members' Sacrifice:

Many organization individuals displayed extensive bravery and selflessness, placing the safety of passengers earlier than their non-public. They labored tirelessly to assist passengers to the lifeboats, even at the risk of their lives. Some institution contributors, like the wi-fi operators Jack Phillips and Harold Bride, continued to ship misery indicators and assist others however knowing that they may now not live to inform the tale.

Passengers' Acts of Courage:

Several passengers proven fantastic bravery and sacrifice, assisting others and supporting in the evacuation efforts. Notably, individuals like Molly Brown and Colonel Archibald Gracie displayed control and braveness in the direction of the disaster.

Chapter 5: Sos And Rescue Efforts

Distress Calls and the Role of the RMS Carpathia

After the Titanic struck the iceberg, the wireless operators, Jack Phillips and Harold Bride, labored tirelessly to deliver out misery signs using the supply's superior wi-fi telegraphy gadget. The alerts, inside the shape of the CQD (Come Quick, Danger) and SOS (Save Our Souls) codes, had been relayed to any nearby ships and land-based totally sincerely stations that could help in the rescue attempt.

The RMS Carpathia Responds:

The closest ship to the Titanic's role changed into the RMS Carpathia, commanded through Captain Arthur Rostron. Upon receiving the Titanic's misery signs, Captain Rostron right away ordered his deliver to trade route and steam at complete speed in the direction of the Titanic's area, which modified into about fifty eight miles away.

The Rescue Effort:

Despite the hard situations, which encompass darkness, frigid waters, and the chance of icebergs, the RMS Carpathia pushed thru the night time time to achieve the Titanic. The team onboard the Carpathia prepared for the rescue operation, readying lifeboats and awesome machine.

Arrival on the Scene:

At approximately 4:00 AM on April 15, 1912, the RMS Carpathia arrived on the vicinity wherein the Titanic had sunk. The Carpathia's enterprise encountered a grim scene with lifeboats scattered inside the water and survivors struggling to stay afloat in the icy Atlantic waters.

Search and Rescue inside the Frigid Atlantic Waters

The rescue operation in the frigid waters of the North Atlantic have emerge as a difficult and daunting project. The organization of the RMS Carpathia displayed wonderful talents and determination in rescuing as many survivors as viable.

Lifeboats and Survivors:

The Carpathia's group right away began out the challenge of selecting up survivors from the lifeboats. They cautiously maneuvered their very non-public lifeboats via the ice-crammed waters, taking on board the freezing and exhausted survivors.

The Struggle to Find More:

Despite their pleasant efforts, the Carpathia's company couldn't locate any extra lifeboats or survivors. The sinking of the Titanic had took place hastily, and the dearth of lifeboats had resulted in a huge loss of life.

Tragic Losses:

Over 1,500 passengers and organization individuals perished within the catastrophe, leaving a heartbreaking toll of lives out of place. The survivors onboard the Carpathia have been shaken through the usage of the tragic occasions that they had witnessed and skilled.

Passenger Reunions and Aftermath

The RMS Carpathia headed closer to New York City with the survivors onboard. The rescue marked the end of the ordeal for folks who have been stored, however their emotional wounds could take a brilliant deal longer to heal.

Passenger Reunions:

Once in New York, the survivors had been met with a combination of emotions, as they had been reunited with their loved ones or faced the grief of dropping family and buddies. The media coverage of the disaster and the survivors' tales made headlines spherical the arena, contributing to the general public's surprise and sorrow.

Inquiries and Investigations:

The sinking of the Titanic delivered about inquiries on both factors of the Atlantic. The

United States Senate convened a completely unique subcommittee to investigate the catastrophe, led through using Senator William Alden Smith. The British Board of Trade furthermore held its own studies.

Changes in Maritime Safety Regulations: The inquiries ended in severa changes to maritime safety pointers. New necessities were implemented for lifeboat potential, lifeboat drills, and the repute quo of 24-hour wireless tracking of distress frequencies. The International Ice Patrol grow to be additionally installed to display icebergs in the North Atlantic.

The sinking of the Titanic remains one of the deadliest maritime screw ups in facts, and its effect on maritime safety hints is profound. The heroism and sacrifice of people onboard, together with the braveness of the RMS Carpathia's group in rescuing survivors, function a testomony to the human spirit in the face of tragedy. The legacy of the Titanic continues to remind us of the significance of prioritizing protection and preparedness within the face of potential screw ups at sea.

Survivors' Tales: Stories of Triumph and Tragedy

Personal Accounts of Survivors

The money owed of survivors of the Titanic's sinking provide a firsthand glimpse into the harrowing activities they persisted on that fateful night time time. Their recollections reflect the priority, courage, and resilience of people who experienced one of the first-rate maritime screw ups in data.

Lawrence Beesley - A Teacher's Tale:

Lawrence Beesley, a second-elegance passenger and a teacher, penned an extensive account of his studies within the ebook "The Loss of the S.S. Titanic." He described the collision and next evacuation, together with the eerie calmness that enveloped the deliver as it sank. Beesley's account supplied valuable insights into the emotions and reactions of passengers at some stage inside the catastrophe.

Archibald Gracie - From Hero to Survivor: Colonel Archibald Gracie, a superb passenger, exhibited first-rate courage and heroism inside the route of the evacuation. He helped others into lifeboats and refused to board one himself till there were no more women to be stored. Eventually, he ended up inside the freezing water and end up later rescued by using way of a lifeboat from the Carpathia.

Charlotte Collyer - A Family's Tragedy: Charlotte Collyer, a third-elegance passenger, endured a heartbreaking ordeal. She out of region her husband, Harvey, at some point of the sinking and end up separated from her younger daughter, Marjorie, all through the chaotic evacuation. Charlotte and Marjorie were in the end reunited aboard the Carpathia.

Jack Thayer - A Survivor's Grief:

Jack Thayer, a 17-one year-antique high-quality passenger, out of region his father within the sinking. He survived with the resource of way of clinging to an overturned collapsible lifeboat and have emerge as sooner or later rescued by way of manner of every other lifeboat. Thayer's account of the catastrophe contemplated the emotional trauma he persisted and the grief he felt over the loss of his father.

Coping with the Trauma: The Mental and Emotional Aftermath

The sinking of the Titanic had a profound and lasting effect on the highbrow and emotional well-being of survivors. Many struggled to address the trauma they professional that night time time and the profound loss of cherished ones.

Survivor's Guilt:

Survivors often grappled with emotions of survivor's guilt, questioning why they were spared while others perished. They carried the load of understanding they survived a disaster that claimed such lots of lives, important to feelings of disappointment and discomfort.

Post-Traumatic Stress:

Many survivors skilled post-traumatic pressure sickness (PTSD), with nightmares, flashbacks, and tension induced thru reminiscences of the catastrophe. The sounds of the supply's distress calls and the sight of icebergs haunted their thoughts for years.

Coping Mechanisms:

In the aftermath of the catastrophe, survivors hired diverse coping mechanisms to deal with their emotional pain. Some sought solace in faith, even as others determined aid via counseling or organization treatment.

Support Networks:

Survivors regularly discovered consolation in connecting with special survivors who shared comparable studies. These connections supplied a steady area for them to manner their emotions and heal from the trauma.

Lifelong Impact:

For many survivors, the emotional effect of the Titanic's sinking persisted inside the direction of their lives. The trauma left an indelible mark on their psyches, influencing their relationships, perspectives, and moves for future years.

The sinking of the Titanic no longer handiest resulted in the loss of lives but additionally left a lasting emotional impact on those who survived. Their non-public debts provide treasured insights into the human revel in inside the route of taken into consideration one of data's maximum tragic disasters. The reminiscences of survival and resilience function a testament to the power of the human spirit in the face of no longer viable adversity.

Chapter 6: Investigations And Inquiries

The Inquiries: The US and British Investigations

Following the sinking of the Titanic, both the usa and the UK done separate investigations to decide the reasons of the catastrophe and to assess the movements of those involved.

United States Senate Inquiry:

The U.S. Senate Commerce Committee held a proper inquiry into the Titanic disaster, which started out out on April 19, 1912, honestly days after the survivors arrived in New York. The inquiry became chaired through Senator William Alden Smith.

Key elements of the U.S. Senate inquiry:

The committee referred to as upon surviving passengers, group participants, and White Star Line officials to offer recollections approximately the events vital as masses due to the fact the collision and the evacuation way. Captain Arthur Rostron of the RMS Carpathia have become additionally known as to testify approximately his supply's reaction and rescue efforts. The feature of the wireless operators and the handling of the iceberg warnings were intently scrutinized within the route of the hearings. The loss of lifeboats and the slow response to the misery signals had been a number of the critical focal factors of the inquiry. British Board of Trade Inquiry:

In the UK, the Board of Trade held its personal inquiry into the Titanic disaster, beginning on May 2, 1912. The British inquiry changed into led via Lord Mersey, moreover called Lord John Charles Bigham.

Key factors of the British Board of Trade inquiry:

Similar to the U.S. Senate inquiry, the British inquiry known as upon survivors, group members, and White Star Line officials to testify. The British inquiry explored the supply's format, production, and protection skills. The trouble of the watertight booths and their failure to increase to the top decks got here beneath scrutiny. The roles of

Captain Edward J. Smith, Chief Officer William Murdoch, and the supply's lookout, Frederick Fleet, had been closely tested finally of the hearings. The conduct of the deliver's wireless operators, Jack Phillips and Harold Bride, became additionally a topic of research. The Blame Game: Evaluating the Verdicts

Both inquiries reached comparable conclusions, attributing the disaster to a aggregate of human blunders, the lack of particular sufficient protection measures, and the excessive tempo at which the Titanic modified into crusing.

The U.S. Senate Inquiry Verdict:

The U.S. Senate inquiry concluded that the disaster modified into in modern-day the stop result of negligence at the a part of the White Star Line and its failure to provide sufficient lifeboats for all passengers and group. The inquiry additionally criticized the coping with of the iceberg warnings and the inadequate response to the misery indicators.

The British Board of Trade Inquiry Verdict: The British inquiry in big factor concurred with the findings of the U.S. Senate inquiry, putting brilliant blame on the dearth of lifeboats and the supply's excessive velocity. However, it additionally held Captain Smith chargeable for now not altering the deliver's course and pace even as ice warnings were acquired.

Additional Factors:

Both inquiries said that the sinking of the Titanic have end up a complex event with a couple of contributing factors. The layout of the deliver, together with the inadequate subdivision of the watertight booths, accomplished a feature in the speedy flooding and next sinking of the vessel.

Ultimately, the inquiries exposed deficiencies in maritime safety hints and taken approximately huge changes in international maritime legal guidelines. The tragedy of the Titanic precipitated the adoption of latest guidelines to ensure the safety of passengers at sea, which includes requirements for enough lifeboats, obligatory lifeboat drills, and non-forestall wi-fi monitoring of misery signs and symptoms. The instructions positioned out from the Titanic's sinking have had a protracted lasting effect on maritime protection practices, aiming to prevent similar screw ups in the destiny.

Legacy of the Titanic: Lessons Learned

Safety Regulations and Maritime Reforms

The sinking of the Titanic had a profound impact on safety regulations and maritime practices, leading to massive reforms geared in the direction of stopping similar disasters inside the future. Governments and maritime corporations round the area carried out a sequence of latest regulations and policies to enhance the safety of passenger ships and beautify emergency preparedness.

International Ice Patrol:

In response to the Titanic catastrophe, the International Ice Patrol end up hooked up.

This company organization, which remains active nowadays, video display gadgets iceberg risks within the North Atlantic delivery lanes in the course of the iceberg season. The patrol issues ice warnings to ships in the area, assisting to save you collisions with icebergs.

SOLAS Convention:

The sinking of the Titanic furthermore accomplished a essential feature within the improvement of the International Convention for the Safety of Life at Sea (SOLAS). The SOLAS Convention is an global maritime treaty that devices minimum safety necessities for passenger and cargo ships. It emerge as first observed in 1914, and next revisions have further improved protection tips for ships.

Lifeboat Capacity Requirements:

The maximum extensive reform because of the Titanic disaster turned into the boom in lifeboat capability on passenger ships. The SOLAS Convention mandated that ships convey sufficient lifeboats to cope with all passengers and group on board. This regulation aimed to make certain that there might be enough lifeboat region to evacuate all and sundry within the occasion of an emergency.

Lifeboat Drills and Safety Training:

Another critical reform come to be the arrival of obligatory lifeboat drills and protection schooling for passengers and business enterprise. All passengers must now take part in lifeboat drills unexpectedly after embarkation to familiarize themselves with the evacuation strategies and the region of lifeboat stations.

Wireless Communications:

The Titanic's wi-fi telegraphy device changed into instrumental in the rescue try, as it enabled the transmission of misery signals and the coordination of rescue operations. After the catastrophe, policies were set up region to make sure that every one passenger ships maintained 24-hour radio watch, which appreciably advanced verbal exchange and emergency reaction competencies.

The Impact on Travel and Ship Design

The sinking of the Titanic profoundly affected the layout and introduction of passenger ships, similarly to the public's perception of ocean excursion.

Enhanced Ship Design and Safety Features: Shipbuilders started out incorporating training found out from the Titanic disaster into the format and production of new vessels. Ships had been built with double hulls, improved watertight cubicles, and strengthened bulkheads to decorate their resistance to flooding in case of a collision.

Passenger Confidence and Demand:

In the aftermath of the Titanic tragedy, there was a quick decline in ocean travel because of heightened public apprehension approximately deliver protection. However, the implementation of latest safety guidelines and the notion that ocean liners had been now extra consistent within the placed up-Titanic era induced a sluggish resurgence in passenger self warranty and speak to for for transatlantic journey.

Iconic Ship Names:

The Titanic catastrophe left an indelible mark on well-known lifestyle and maritime records. The call "Titanic" have become synonymous with every the magnificence of high-priced ocean liners and the tragedy of maritime disasters. As a stop cease end result, many next ships were named after the Titanic to evoke a experience of grandeur and reverence for maritime history.

Innovations in Emergency Procedures:

The catastrophe moreover caused improvements in emergency strategies and protocols for passenger ships. The development of entire emergency plans, evacuation techniques, and coordination with rescue services have emerge as a massive exercise for the maritime enterprise.

The legacy of the Titanic remains a powerful reminder of the importance of safety in ocean adventure. The reforms and changes applied after the catastrophe have considerably advanced maritime safety and maintain to influence deliver layout and operational practices to at the present time. The story of the Titanic continues to captivate the general public's creativeness, serving as a poignant reminder of the importance of mastering from past tragedies to construct a more steady destiny for maritime tour.

Chapter 7: Titanic In Popular Culture

Literature and Films: Keeping the Legend Alive

The story of the Titanic has captured the public's creativeness for over a century, inspiring limitless works of literature and movies that have helped immortalize the supply's legend.

Literature

Numerous books, each fiction and non-fiction, have been written approximately the Titanic. Some amazing works consist of:

"A Night to Remember" via Walter Lord: A gripping and entire non-fiction account of the Titanic's sinking, drawing intently on survivor memories and ancient information.

"Titanic" thru the usage of James Cameron: A novelization of the blockbuster movie directed through James Cameron. The ebook expands at the characters and activities depicted within the movie.

"The Deep" through Peter Benchley: A novel that capabilities a plot focused around the discovery of the Titanic's wreckage in current-day instances, intertwining historic factors with fictional storytelling.

Films

The tale of the Titanic has been tailored into severa films, every imparting a totally precise attitude at the catastrophe and its impact. Some of the maximum splendid Titanic films include:

"A Night to Remember" (1958): Directed via Roy Ward Baker, this British movie is based totally mostly on Walter Lord's e-book and is considered one of the maximum correct depictions of the disaster.

"Titanic" (1997): Directed with the beneficial useful resource of James Cameron, this epic romance movie have become one of the maximum-grossing movies of all time. While it includes fictional characters and a love story, it moreover highlights the historic factors of the tragedy.

"Titanic" (1953): Directed with the useful resource of Jean Negulesco, this film is a traditional romantic drama starring Barbara Stanwyck and Clifton Webb. It fictionalizes the events principal as an lousy lot because the catastrophe.

Music and Art: Immortalizing the Titanic's Story

The Titanic's tale has also left a big effect at the area of track and artwork, with severa compositions, art work, and sculptures commemorating the deliver and its passengers.

Music

The sinking of the Titanic has been the foundation for numerous musical compositions:

"Nearer, My God, to Thee": This hymn have emerge as reportedly done via the deliver's musicians at a few level inside the very last moments in advance than the Titanic sank. It has become cautiously related to the catastrophe.

"My Heart Will Go On": This song, sung through Celine Dion, served because the subject track for James Cameron's 1997 film "Titanic." The music's powerful lyrics and emotional melody captured the hearts of heaps and hundreds international.

Art

The Titanic has been the issue of severa paintings and artworks, taking images the supply in all its grandeur and at some stage in its tragic sinking. These works of paintings often evoke the drama, heroism, and loss associated with the disaster.

"The Sinking of the Titanic" through Willy Stöwer: A dramatic painting depicting the deliver sinking and lifeboats full of survivors.

"The Wreck of the Titan" via George Spencer Melvin: A portray that foreshadows the sinking of a fictional supply named "Titan" strikingly much like the Titanic.

These literary and artistic works have helped keep the legend of the Titanic alive, ensuring that the story and its commands are exceeded down through generations. They characteristic a poignant reminder of the deliver's grandeur, the tragedy that opened up on that fateful night time, and the enduring impact of one of the maximum notorious maritime screw ups in history.

The discovery of the Titanic's wreckage have come to be a huge historical event and a testament to human ingenuity and resolution. For many years, the vicinity of the deliver's very last resting place remained a thriller, until severa expeditions in the end placed the wreckage.

Early Efforts:

Several expeditions within the years following the Titanic's sinking tried to discover the wreckage but had been unsuccessful because of the vastness of the North Atlantic and the regulations of available technology.

Dr. Robert Ballard's Discovery:

In September 1985, a joint French-American day trip, led with the aid of the use of manner of Dr. Robert Ballard, in the end positioned the Titanic's wreckage. Using advanced sonar generation and remotely operated underwater automobiles (ROVs), the institution decided the supply's stays resting on the sea ground at a intensity of about 12,500 toes (3,800 meters).

Chapter 8: Memorials And Memorabilia

Memorial Services and Tributes

In the wake of the Titanic catastrophe, memorial services and tributes have been held to honor the reminiscence of people who perished. These ceremonies furnished an possibility for grieving households and organizations to go returned collectively and pay their respects.

St. Paul's Cathedral Memorial Service:

One of the maximum excellent memorial services occurred at St. Paul's Cathedral in London on April 19, 1912. The service emerge as attended through dignitaries, survivors, and families of the patients. It became a somber event that brought together people from unique walks of existence to mourn and keep in mind the lives out of vicinity.

Other Memorial Services:

Memorial services had been additionally held in diverse towns and towns throughout the United Kingdom, the USA, and particular countries. These offerings had been attended with the useful resource of lots, offering a collective 2nd of grief and remembrance.

Titanic Memorial Garden:

In Belfast, Northern Ireland, in which the Titanic become constructed, a memorial garden become created in honor of the supply and its passengers. The garden capabilities plaques with the names of folks who perished and serves as a peaceful space for reflected image.

Individual Memorials:

Many families erected person memorials for their lost cherished ones. These memorials can be positioned in cemeteries and public regions round the vicinity, each supplying a poignant reminder of the private toll the disaster took on households.

Titanic Memorabilia and Collectibles

The Titanic disaster has furthermore given upward thrust to a extensive market for

Titanic memorabilia and collectibles. Items associated with the ship, its passengers, and the activities of that tragic night time time are pretty famous through lenders and enthusiasts.

Newspapers and Magazines:

Newspapers and magazines posted particular variations reporting at the disaster. Original copies of those guides have become valuable collectibles, providing a firsthand account of the events as they spread out.

Postcards and Photographs:

Postcards and images of the Titanic earlier than its fateful voyage, as well as snap shots of the shipwreck and the recovery of artifacts, are famous among creditors. Some of those devices are unusual and fantastically prized.

Titanic Passenger and Crew Lists:

Reproductions or proper passenger and group lists from the Titanic's maiden voyage are in name for through creditors inquisitive about tracing the names of unique people who have been onboard.

Artifacts and Ship Fittings:

Some actual artifacts recovered from the Titanic, which includes china, silverware, and deliver fittings, have been offered at auctions and are pretty valued via lenders. There is likewise a marketplace for real gadgets from the deliver's sister ships, the Olympic and the Britannic.

Movie Memorabilia:

Items related to the 1997 film "Titanic," which includes movie posters, merchandise, and props used inside the movie, have grow to be famous collectibles among fans of the movie.

It is important to have a look at that at the same time as Titanic memorabilia can be thrilling and traditionally considerable, there are also many reproductions and fake objects in the marketplace. Collectors and lovers should exercising caution and studies the authenticity of gadgets earlier than making purchases. Additionally, a few view the commercialization of Titanic memorabilia as arguable because of the sensitive nature of the tragedy.

Myths and Misconceptions: Separating Fact from Fiction

Debunking Popular Myths Surrounding the Titanic

The sinking of the Titanic has given rise to severa myths and misconceptions over time. Let's find out a number of the most commonplace myths and set the report without delay with the information:

Myth: The Titanic modified into the primary supply to use the "SOS" distress signal. Fact: The Titanic's distress sign come to be clearly "CQD" ("Come Quick, Danger") and not "SOS." While "CQD" turn out to be in not unusual use on the time, the Titanic's wi-fi operators additionally transmitted the newly observed "SOS" check in a few unspecified time inside the future of the catastrophe.

Myth: The band carried out "Nearer, My God, to Thee" due to the truth the ship sank. Fact: The band did play track at some point of the evacuation to calm passengers, however there may be uncertainty approximately the precise tunes executed. Some survivors recalled paying attention to "Nearer, My God, to Thee," even as others stated specific songs.

Myth: The lifeboats had been not filled to capacity at some degree within the evacuation. Fact: While some lifeboats had been not crammed to their most functionality, it wasn't because of a lack of scenario for passengers. Some lifeboats were decreased with just a few passengers onboard, as team people had been unsure in their capability to soundly navigate the boat on the identical time as without a doubt loaded.

Myth: The supply turned into touring at whole pace even as it hit the iceberg. Fact: The Titanic turn out to be now not travelling at entire tempo on the time of the collision. The deliver's officials had acquired numerous iceberg warnings and had already reduced the speed to navigate via the ice state of affairs thoroughly.

The Truth Behind Titanic's "Unsinkable" Reputation

The Titanic's popularity as "unsinkable" turned into no longer a claim made with the useful resource of the supply's builders, however alternatively a belief that emerged in the media and some of the general public on the time. The false impression can be traced lower again to severa factors:

Advanced Safety Features:

The Titanic become taken into consideration an engineering surprise and modified into equipped with advanced safety capabilities for its time, which includes watertight cubicles and an intensive double-bottom hull. These talents have been supposed to decorate the deliver's survivability inside the event of a collision.

Media Hype:

The White Star Line and media shops closely promoted the Titanic as a picture of steeply-priced and technological superiority. The supply's opulence, mixed with the perception of its superior safety skills, brought about the belief that it changed into definitely unsinkable.

Limited Lifeboat Capacity:

Despite its protection capabilities, the Titanic's layout despite the fact that had big vulnerabilities, together with a restrained sort of lifeboats. While it surpassed the regulations of the time, the deliver's lifeboat capability grow to be insufficient to residence all passengers and crew.

Human Error:

The remaining purpose of the Titanic's sinking became the human mistakes that delivered about the collision with the iceberg. The supply's officers did not take immediately and powerful motion to keep away from the iceberg, contributing to the catastrophe.

The sinking of the Titanic shattered the notion in its invincibility and had a profound effect on maritime protection recommendations. The tragedy exposed the want for stricter safety standards, along with sufficient lifeboat capability, advanced conversation structures, and higher schooling for team members. The legacy of the Titanic continues to feature a reminder that even the maximum superior generation can be liable to human mistakes and that safety want to continuously be a top priority in maritime excursion.

Chapter 9: The Olympic And Britannic

The White Star Line, the commercial enterprise agency that owned the Titanic, had numerous extraordinary vessels in its fleet, two of the most top notch being the Olympic and the Britannic. Here's a brief assessment in their fates:

RMS Olympic:

The RMS Olympic changed into the primary of the three Olympic-beauty ocean liners built for the White Star Line. It became the sister supply of the Titanic, sharing a similar layout and masses of functions. The Olympic have become launched on October 20, 1910, and entered provider in 1911.

Fate of the RMS Olympic:

The Olympic had an extended and eventful career as a passenger liner. Unlike her ill-fated sister, the Titanic, the Olympic loved a success service life. She endured strolling for over some years, serving in some unspecified time in the future of World War I as a troopship and returning to industrial organisation company later on.

In 1934, the Olympic changed into worried in a collision with the Nantucket lightship off the coast of Massachusetts. The twist of fate resulted inside the lack of the lightship and a few damage to the Olympic's bow, but she turned into repaired and endured provider.

As the age of ocean liners waned due to the rise of air tour, the Olympic's characteristic as a passenger supply dwindled. She became finally withdrawn from provider and scrapped in 1937.

HMHS Britannic:

The HMHS Britannic turn out to be the 0.33 and biggest of the Olympic-class liners. Initially constructed to be a passenger liner like her sisters, the Britannic became requisitioned thru the British government for the duration of World War I to function a health center deliver.

Fate of the HMHS Britannic:

On November 21, 1916, at the identical time as serving as a health center supply in the Mediterranean, the Britannic struck a mine laid with the useful resource of a German submarine off the coast of the Greek island of Kea. The deliver sank hastily, however not much like the Titanic, the crew's fast reaction and the presence of lifeboats and lifestyles rafts stored many lives.

Out of the approximately 1,100 humans onboard, 30 misplaced their lives within the catastrophe. The Britannic's destroy now lies at a depth of spherical four hundred toes (one hundred twenty meters) on the seabed, making it a well-known vacation spot for divers and maritime archaeologists.

The future of the Olympic and the Britannic serves as a reminder of the risks and demanding situations faced by manner of ocean liners all through the early 20th century. Despite the tragic sinking of the Titanic, each vessels had numerous careers and contributed substantially to maritime facts.

Titanic Artifacts: Preserving the Past

Recovered Artifacts and Their Preservation

The exploration of the Titanic destroy web web website has yielded a exceptional huge style of artifacts, imparting a tangible connection to the deliver and its passengers. Preserving the ones artifacts is a sensitive method because of the unique conditions of the break web web page and the fragility of the devices themselves.

Recovery Efforts:

Numerous expeditions were achieved to the Titanic wreck website to get higher artifacts. These objects variety from non-public property, china, and supply fittings to massive pieces of the deliver's shape.

Conservation and Preservation:

Once recovered, the artifacts go through a meticulous conservation way. The devices are treated to dispose of salt and one-of-a-kind impurities, and they may be carefully saved in controlled environments to prevent further deterioration.

Exhibition Partnerships:

Some artifacts were placed on display in museums and exhibitions worldwide. In in many instances, the ones exhibitions are made feasible thru partnerships among non-public salvage agencies, authorities agencies, and museums.

Museums and Exhibitions: Showcasing Titanic History

Exhibitions devoted to the Titanic provide an opportunity for the general public to learn about the ship's statistics, the catastrophe, and the lives of those onboard. These exhibitions often include a mixture of artifacts, historical records, interactive suggests, and multimedia presentations.

Titanic Belfast, Northern Ireland:

Located inside the birthplace of the Titanic, Titanic Belfast is a worldwide-elegance museum and tourist appeal that tells the tale of the supply's advent, launch, and tragic stop. It houses numerous artifacts and interactive reveals, imparting traffic an entire and immersive enjoy.

National Maritime Museum, Greenwich, London: The National Maritime Museum features a Titanic-associated exhibition, showing artifacts and private gadgets recovered from the break. The exhibition offers insights into the passengers' critiques and the effect of the catastrophe.

Titanic Museum, Pigeon Forge, Tennessee, and Branson, Missouri, USA: These privately-owned museums in the United States display off artifacts, replicas, and interactive reveals, inviting traffic to step once more in time and revel in the Titanic's adventure.

Traveling Exhibitions:

Some Titanic exhibitions are designed to adventure to special towns and international locations, allowing a broader target marketplace to experience the data and artifacts related to the Titanic.

Preserving the artifacts recovered from the Titanic is of most importance, as they are tangible hyperlinks to a huge moment in records. By showcasing the ones artifacts in museums and exhibitions, human beings from round the arena can discover approximately the Titanic's legacy, the human memories at the back of the catastrophe, and the training it has taught us about maritime safety and information.

Chapter 10: A Timeless Legend

Visiting Titanic's Final Resting Place

The Titanic's very last resting place is located approximately 370 miles (six hundred kilometers) southeast of Newfoundland, Canada, at a depth of spherical 12,500 feet (three,800 meters). The website on-line is one of the most massive underwater archaeological websites in records. However, traveling the damage is a challenging and complex company because of the intense depth and a long way flung place of the internet web page.

Expeditions to the Wreck:

Numerous expeditions have been conducted to the Titanic wreck internet web website thinking about that its discovery in 1985. These expeditions have used modern-day submersibles and remotely operated automobiles (ROVs) to discover and report the break.

Deep-Sea Submersibles:

State-of-the-art deep-sea submersibles, which encompass the Russian MIR submersibles and the American Alvin, have been used to transport researchers and explorers to the depths of the damage net web page. These submersibles are able to withstanding the wonderful stress of the deep ocean.

Remote Operated Vehicles (ROVs):

ROVs prepared with excessive-definition cameras and robot fingers are used to seize unique pictures and accumulate samples from the damage. These motors permit researchers to check the net internet page with out physical descending to the depths themselves.

Challenges and Risks:

Visiting the Titanic break isn't always without dangers. The some distance flung region and extreme intensity of the net website present logistical demanding situations, and the harm itself is deteriorating over the years because of the corrosive outcomes of the deep-sea environment.

Conservation and Preservation:

Efforts to go to the Titanic damage are finished with a strong emphasis on conservation and safety. Researchers and explorers must adhere to strict guidelines to keep away from damaging the internet site or disposing of artifacts.

Future Visits:

Future visits to the Titanic destroy will probably stay restrained because of the need to stability exploration with renovation. New generation and enhancements in deep-sea exploration may also moreover offer further opportunities for researchers and explorers to study the ruin on the identical time as respecting its ancient importance.

The Titanic's Enduring Symbolism

The Titanic's enduring symbolism lies in its reputation as a powerful reminder of human vulnerability and the consequences of hubris. The disaster serves as a poignant cautionary story approximately the restrictions of generation and the significance of prioritizing protection over grandeur.

Human Tragedy:

The sinking of the Titanic resulted within the lack of over 1,500 lives, making it one of the deadliest peacetime maritime disasters in statistics. The human toll of the tragedy has left an indelible mark at the collective memory and keeps to rouse feelings of grief and empathy.

Chapter 11: A Symbol Of Human Hubris And Resilience

The Tragic Irony of the "Unsinkable" Ship

The Titanic's tragic irony lies within the stark evaluation amongst its recognition as an "unsinkable" deliver and its actual future. The belief that the Titanic modified into invincible changed into not a claim made through its builders however as a substitute a belief that emerged inside the media and among the public. This notion come to be fueled thru the supply's superior safety functions, luxurious centers, and the White Star Line's promotional efforts.

The Titanic have become heralded as a technological wonder and the epitome of costly and opulence. Its designers covered advanced protection functions along facet watertight booths and a double-backside hull, which have been believed to make the supply in reality unsinkable. The hubris surrounding the Titanic grow to be in addition fueled by way of the perception that its advanced abilities, blended with the enjoy of its group, must control any state of affairs that might upward thrust up.

However, the sinking of the Titanic on its maiden voyage shattered this perception. The supply's collision with an iceberg on the night time of April 14, 1912, led to a catastrophic failure of its protection measures. The watertight booths did now not amplify far sufficient to prevent flooding, and the collision introduced about a sequence of punctures that triggered the deliver's slow sinking.

Lessons in Human Hubris

The tragedy of the Titanic serves as a powerful lesson in human hubris and the risks of overconfidence. The perception in the Titanic's invincibility blinded its designers and operators to the capacity dangers and vulnerabilities that existed. It underscores the significance of humility, careful chance evaluation, and an understanding of the regulations of era.

The sinking of the Titanic found the effects of human complacency and the dangers of brushing off capability threats. The disaster highlighted the want for non-stop vigilance, thorough protection measures, and a willingness to research from past mistakes.

Strength of the Human Spirit

Despite the devastating lack of lifestyles, the Titanic disaster moreover showcased the fantastic power of the human spirit. In the face of a catastrophic state of affairs, many passengers and crew individuals displayed acts of bravery, compassion, and self-sacrifice.

The deliver's team labored tirelessly to evacuate passengers and launch lifeboats, regularly placing the protection of others before their very very own. Passengers helped each other, and some sacrificed their very very personal possibilities of survival to make sure that others had a better hazard of creating it to safety.

The survivors' debts of heroism and resilience amidst tragedy have become a long lasting a part of the Titanic's legacy. Their tales remind us of the capability of the human spirit to bear and act with braveness within the most difficult conditions.

Ultimately, the Titanic's tragic irony serves as a reminder that human endeavors, regardless of how grand or bold, aren't resistant to the forces of nature and unexpected occasions. The lessons of the Titanic preserve to resonate, prompting us to technique our endeavors with humility, foresight, and an unwavering dedication to the safety and nicely-being of others. At the equal time, the energy and resilience displayed via the use of way of those on board the Titanic remind us of the indomitable spirit this is living inner humanity, inspiring us to stand adversity with courage and compassion.

Remembering the Titanic: Personal Reflections

The sinking of the Titanic over a century ago maintains to have a profound and enduring effect on society and life-style. The reasons why we hold to hold in thoughts the Titanic can be attributed to severa key factors:

Human Tragedy and Loss:

The Titanic's sinking resulted within the loss of greater than 1,500 lives, making it one of the deadliest peacetime maritime failures in facts. The sheer scale of the human tragedy and the dearth of lives, collectively with humans from diverse social backgrounds and nationalities, struck a chord with people across the arena.

Stories of Heroism and Sacrifice:

The Titanic's disaster additionally brought forth recollections of heroism and sacrifice, as passengers and crew people labored to keep others amidst the chaos. These recollections of braveness and selflessness have turn out to be an crucial a part of the Titanic's legacy, resonating with audiences and galvanizing a experience of admiration for the human spirit.

Technological Hubris and Lessons in Safety: The Titanic's sinking uncovered the fallibility of human judgment and the risks of setting immoderate confidence in generation. The catastrophe caused massive enhancements in maritime safety rules and supply design, leaving an extended-lasting impact on the delivery employer.

Art and Literature:

The Titanic's story has been immortalized via numerous works of art, literature, and movie. Books, movies, and innovative endeavors that depict the Titanic's tragedy and its impact on society have contributed to its enduring cultural significance.

Exploration and Discovery:

The discovery of the Titanic break in 1985 sparked public hobby in underwater archaeology and deep-sea exploration. The exploration of the smash and the recuperation of artifacts have introduced a experience of mystery and wonder to the Titanic's story.

Symbol of Lost Dreams:

The Titanic represented the aspirations of an era characterised with the aid of way of development and modernity. Its tragic surrender stands as a picture of the fragility of human goals and the unpredictability of future.

Commemoration and Remembrance:

Anniversary commemorations, memorials, and activities maintain to keep the reminiscence of the Titanic alive inside the public recognition. These occasions offer an opportunity for reflected image, honoring the lives lost, and getting to know from statistics.

Chapter 12: The Unsinkable Ship Myths And Realities

The Titanic, often hailed as "unsinkable," has grown to be a surprise of its time. In this financial ruin, we can find out the myths and realities surrounding the deliver's advent and layout. We'll delve into the bold claims made approximately the deliver's invincibility, the modern-day era that have been presupposed to preserve it afloat, and the elements that contributed to the parable of the "unsinkable" Titanic.

The early twentieth century turned into a length of awesome advancements in shipbuilding and technology, and the Titanic turned into the top of these achievements. As we adventure again in time, we are able to discover the ambition and imaginative and prescient that went into growing this brilliant vessel.

The Vision of Titanic

The concept of the Titanic changed into born from the minds of a number of the maximum visionary people of the time. The deliver changed into a part of a trio, along the RMS Olympic and HMHS Britannic, collectively referred to as the Olympic-elegance liners. These ships have been designed to provide amazing steeply-priced and safety for passengers touring at some stage in the Atlantic.

The concept of an unsinkable ship changed into no longer a mere advertising and advertising ploy; it grow to be a reflected picture of the generation's believe in era and engineering. The designers of the Titanic incorporated advanced protection capabilities, which include a double hull and severa watertight booths. The supply's creators believed that even within the occasion of a collision, the Titanic must live afloat, ensuring the safety of its passengers.

The Illusion of Invincibility

The White Star Line, the company in the back of the Titanic, spared no value in selling the supply's invincibility. The media of the time eagerly echoed the belief of the "unsinkable" ship. Newspapers and magazines carried tales about the grandeur of the vessel and the opulence of its indoors. The Titanic changed into designed to be a floating palace, and the world could not help however be captivated through manner of it.

As the Titanic's production superior, the myth of its invincibility grew. People began to bear in mind that it changed into not best a deliver however an unsinkable fortress. It's critical to understand that this notion wasn't absolutely driven via arrogance; it was a pondered image of the optimism and recall in improvement that characterized the technology.

Innovations on Board

The Titanic brought numerous groundbreaking features that had been considered innovative at the time. From its advanced communique structures, which includes the Marconi wireless telegraph, to the opulent interiors featuring grand staircases, costly cabins, and a world-class eating experience, the deliver became designed to redefine journey across the Atlantic.

These innovations had been a testament to the human spirit's capability to triumph over the elements and offer consolation and safety. In a unexpectedly evolving worldwide, the Titanic was a image of improvement and luxury.

A Prelude to Tragedy

However, as we are able to explore within the following chapters, this unwavering self guarantee in the Titanic's invincibility may display to be tragically out of place. Despite its technological improvements, the deliver became not proof closer to the forces of nature. The collision with an iceberg on that fateful night time time in April 1912 shattered the myth of the unsinkable ship and despatched shockwaves around the arena.

In unraveling the myths and realities of the Titanic's production and layout, we gain a deeper expertise of the backdrop in opposition to which this epic tale of tragedy and heroism unfolds. This financial disaster is actually the beginning of our journey into the coronary coronary coronary heart of the Titanic's tale.

Titanic's Ill-Fated Maiden Voyage

In this economic ruin, we delve into the begin of the Titanic's journey, the anticipation and pride that surrounded its maiden voyage, and the ominous signs and symptoms that foreshadowed the tragic sports that lay ahead.

A Grand Departure

The Titanic set sail from Southampton, England, on April 10, 1912, with superb fanfare. Crowds accrued to witness the departure of the "supply of dreams." The passengers, a combination of the rich elite and those searching for a current life in America, boarded with excessive expectancies. The ship's opulent indoors and cutting-edge day facilities promised a costly and cushty adventure.

The atmosphere aboard the Titanic became one in every of opulence and luxury. Passengers loved extremely good eating, live tune, and a number of leisure sports activities activities. The ship's format, often in assessment to a floating lodge, aimed to make the voyage a memorable experience for all on board.

The Route to Disaster

As the Titanic launched into its maiden voyage, it located a northern direction at some point of the Atlantic, on the lookout for to keep away from icebergs. Despite warnings of ice inside the place, the deliver's captain, Edward J. Smith, and his organization had been assured in the deliver's ability to navigate efficaciously.

However, the winning thoughts-set of invincibility, coupled with the lack of binoculars for the lookout team, proved to be deadly oversights. On the night time of April 14, 1912, the Titanic struck an iceberg. The collision, even though no longer proper now catastrophic, inflicted deadly harm below the waterline, important to the gradual and inexorable sinking of the supply.

Panic and Heroism

As news of the iceberg collision spread in a few unspecified time in the destiny of the supply, panic and confusion gripped the passengers and institution. While there were inadequate lifeboats for all aboard, many struggled to come back to phrases with the reality that the "unsinkable" Titanic turn out to be in grave danger.

Chapter 13: The Passengers Aboard Titanic

As we preserve our journey into the coronary coronary heart of the Titanic's tale, we turn our hobby to the diverse and captivating array of passengers who launched into this sick-fated maiden voyage. From the wealthiest human beings of the era to the hopeful immigrants searching out a better life in America, the Titanic's passengers represented a skip-section of early 20th-century society.

A Microcosm of Society

The Titanic's passenger listing modified right into a microcosm of the societal divisions of the time. The deliver's take place covered some of the wealthiest and maximum distinguished individuals of the era, collectively with John Jacob Astor IV, Benjamin Guggenheim, and Isidor Straus. These extraordinary passengers cherished the peak of costly and privilege aboard the supply.

In comparison, the 1/3-class passengers, a variety of whom had been immigrants, sought a brighter future in America. They traveled in extra modest lodges, however their adventure changed into no lots less substantial. The Titanic represented the opportunity for a smooth start, and their hopes have been as high as those in their best opposite numbers.

Personal Stories and Aspirations

Each passenger had their very very own specific tale and aspiration. For some, the voyage emerge as a holiday of an entire lifestyles, an possibility to bask within the opulence of the deliver. For others, it became a technique of pursuing new business employer possibilities or reuniting with circle of relatives participants remote places.

The Titanic's passengers got here from severa backgrounds, with superb nationalities, professions, and dreams. Some were honeymooners, while others have been kids visiting with their households. The type of the passenger listing highlights the interconnectedness of human lives and the shared destiny that awaited them.

Tragic Endings and Lost Dreams

The tragedy of the Titanic is made all of the more poignant whilst we recollect the misplaced capacity and desires of its passengers. The collision with the iceberg shattered the phantasm of protection and privilege, as passengers from all commands faced the same frightening fact.

As we delve deeper into the private memories of the Titanic's passengers, we're going to come upon acts of bravery, sacrifice, and heartbreak. The selections they made and the situations they confronted could for all time be etched within the annals of records.

In the chapters that take a look at, we are capable of discover a number of the maximum notable man or woman testimonies, from the heroes who gave their lives to shop others to the survivors who carried the reminiscence of that fateful night time with them for the rest in their lives. The passengers of the Titanic remind us that interior every call at the passenger listing, there may be a very precise and compelling tale that deserves to be heard.

The Crew of Titanic: Heroes and Sacrifices

In this bankruptcy, we shift our cognizance to the dedicated group members who executed a critical position in the Titanic's sick-fated adventure. Their unwavering determination, sacrifices, and heroism in the face of an coming close to catastrophe have been instrumental in the survival of many passengers.

The Backbone of the Ship

The organisation of the Titanic consisted of over 800 humans, every with a selected role and duty. From the officers who navigated the supply to the stewards who attended to the passengers' wishes, the enterprise changed into the spine of the vessel's operation.

Captain Edward J. Smith, who had a long and distinguished profession at sea, led the Titanic. His revel in have turn out to be considered unparalleled, and he have grow to be entrusted with the maiden voyage of the deliver, overseeing the operation with self assure and authority.

Heroic Acts of Sacrifice

When disaster struck and the deliver collided with the iceberg, the crew's reaction have become a testament to their education and determination. Many organization human beings labored tirelessly to load lifeboats, making sure the safety of the passengers. They faced excessive situations, which incorporates freezing temperatures and a sense of impending doom, however they persevered their efforts to preserve order and decrease panic.

Some institution contributors, like Captain Smith, Chief Officer William Murdoch, and Chief Engineer Joseph Bell, displayed incredible bravery in the face of adversity. Their moves, in spite of the truth that in the long run in vain, saved lives and exemplified the remarkable requirements of duty and honor.

A Heavy Toll

Tragically, the group of the Titanic did now not break out the disaster unscathed. Many group individuals perished inside the line of responsibility, on the equal time as others fought to stay on within the icy waters of the North Atlantic. The sacrifices made via way of manner of those individuals are a testomony to the heroism and selflessness that emerged in the face of drawing near tragedy.

The Legacy of the Crew

The organization of the Titanic left in the back of a legacy of sacrifice and duty that has turn out to be an essential part of the ship's tale.

Their moves throughout the catastrophe continue to be remembered and honored, serving as a photo of the human ability for braveness and sacrifice in instances of disaster.

As we maintain with our exploration of the Titanic's adventure, we are capable of maintain to stumble upon the testimonies of every passengers and institution, each contributing to the wealthy tapestry of this historic and tragic event. The group's unwavering self-control, regularly inside the face of excellent doom, is a testament to the strength of the human spirit.

Titanic's Grandeur: A Closer Look on the Ship

As we maintain to unravel the tale of the Titanic, we shift our reputation to the grandeur and complicated information of the deliver itself. This bankruptcy gives an in-intensity exploration of the Titanic's opulent interiors, advanced functions, and the sheer elegance of this engineering wonder.

A Floating Palace

The Titanic grow to be designed to be the epitome of luxury and class. Its interiors were a combination of Edwardian splendor and modern innovation. From the instant passengers stepped on board, they had been enveloped in a global of opulence.

The ship's exceptional resorts had been a reflected photograph of the era's top-elegance life-style. Lavish cabins, embellished with notable woodwork and high priced fixtures, furnished a diploma of comfort and fashion extremely good at the time. The grand staircase, with its okaypaneling and hard wrought iron, have become an iconic image of the deliver's grandeur.

A Feast for the Senses

The Titanic's ingesting experience become a culinary masterpiece. First-magnificence passengers dined in a steeply-priced consuming saloon adorned with ornate woodwork and stylish decor. The deliver's à l.

A. Carte restaurant furnished gourmand cuisine, catering to even the most discerning palates.

The 2nd-elegance and 1/3-beauty resorts, at the same time as lots much less extravagant, nonetheless provided a level of comfort and offerings that have been rare on transatlantic voyages. The deliver's designers aimed to make certain that passengers in each elegance felt they had been a part of some issue amazing.

Cutting-Edge Technology

The Titanic have become now not only a palace; it have become additionally a technological wonder of its time. The supply modified into geared up with the cutting-edge upgrades in communication and safety. The Marconi wi-fi telegraph tool allowed for actual-time verbal exchange with the out of doors worldwide, and the supply's superior watertight cubicles had been designed to decorate safety.

However, as we are able to find out within the following chapters, even the most contemporary generation could not prevent the tragic final consequences that awaited the Titanic.

The Art of Preservation

Preserving the Titanic's legacy is an ongoing try. The deliver's grandeur, even in its submerged country on the ocean ground, continues to captivate the area. Many artifacts from the deliver had been recovered and are displayed in museums, permitting us to glimpse into the beyond and respect the craftsmanship and comfort that were as soon as a part of the Titanic.

In this chapter, we have taken a higher observe the grandeur and hard information of the Titanic, putting the quantity for our persevered journey into the coronary coronary heart of this splendid tale. As we delve further into the occasions of that fateful night time in April 1912, we are capable of see how the deliver's splendor and innovation have been in the long run overshadowed thru the tragedy that spread out.

Chapter 14: The Night The Titanic Sank

In this bankruptcy, we navigate the pivotal moments of the Titanic's unwell-fated voyage as catastrophe struck at the cold, moonless night time of April 14, 1912. The collision with the iceberg and the subsequent activities would possibly all the time adjust the course of the deliver's information.

The Deadly Encounter

The night time was calm and easy, and the Titanic glided thru the icy waters of the North Atlantic. The crew remained vigilant for signs and symptoms of ice, but the apparently tranquil situations masked the peril that lay below the floor. At about 11:forty PM, the lookout inside the crow's nest determined an iceberg useless ahead.

Despite instant efforts to steer easy of the iceberg, the brilliant duration of the supply and the iceberg's proximity made a collision inevitable. The impact modified into felt as a shudder at some stage in the delivery, but many passengers were ignorant of the gravity of the state of affairs at that second.

Below the Waterline

The iceberg had torn a series of lethal gashes along the deliver's starboard aspect, beneath the waterline. Water started out out to flood the deliver's booths, and the actual amount of the harm brief have turn out to be obvious to the supply's institution and officers.

Captain Edward J. Smith changed into alerted and right now began out out assessing the situation. Distress indicators had been sent out via the Marconi wireless telegraph, and efforts to find out the overall quantity of the harm have been initiated. As the ship's booths full of water, it commenced to list ahead and to the right.

Evacuation Begins

As the reality of the state of affairs set in, passengers and institution started the method of evacuating the supply. Lifeboats were decreased into the freezing waters of the North Atlantic. The scarcity of lifeboats, mixed with a lack of preparedness and education for such an emergency, would in all likelihood display to be a big assignment in the evacuation efforts.

In this bankruptcy, we've were given explored the important moments even as the Titanic's destiny became sealed with the aid of using the iceberg collision. The night time modified into marked through using confusion, heroism, and tragedy, as passengers and institution grappled with the stark fact that the "unsinkable" Titanic have become in grave threat.

As we preserve with our exploration of this historic event, we are able to delve deeper into the chaos and bravado that defined the hours following the collision, ultimately shaping the path of the Titanic's very last hours.

Lifeboats and Survival

As the Titanic's passengers and group grappled with the awful reality of the collision with the iceberg, this financial ruin makes a speciality of the important factors of lifeboats and the struggle for survival. It explores the challenges confronted at a few diploma in the evacuation and the choices made that might decide the destiny of those on board.

The Shortage of Lifeboats

One of the most placing and tragic components of the Titanic catastrophe have become the inadequate quantity of lifeboats. The supply grow to be organized with simplest sufficient lifeboats to carry approximately half of of of the passengers and organization. This deficiency ought to show catastrophic in the moments following the collision.

The preliminary response to reducing the lifeboats became hesitant and disorganized, as passengers and enterprise struggled to recognize the significance of the state of affairs. Many lifeboats were launched with a protracted way fewer occupants than they may have as it should be carried, leaving empty seats at the same time as others desperately sought an area of safe haven.

Acts of Heroism

Amid the chaos and confusion, acts of heroism emerged. Crew people and passengers worked tirelessly to load lifeboats and hold a semblance of order. Men willingly stepped apart to permit women and children to board, and lots of human beings displayed extremely good bravery inside the face of advantageous peril.

One brilliant example have become the supply's leader wi-fi operator, Jack Phillips, and his assistant, Harold Bride. They remained at their posts, sending distress signs thru wireless telegraph till the very surrender. Their strength of mind and sacrifice might ultimately result in the rescue of survivors by way of the use of close by ships.

The Agonizing Wait

For those left on board, the situation grew increasingly dire. As the Titanic continued to listing and plunge deeper into the frigid waters, the belief that rescue come to be no longer in all likelihood dawned on folks who remained. The sounds of the ship's band gambling tune to calm and luxury the passengers echoed through the night time.

The economic disaster ends with the haunting scene of the Titanic's stern growing into the night time time sky in advance than plunging under the waves. The deliver's lighting fixtures diminished and people left on board faced a dark, icy fate.

The evacuation and the conflict for survival on the Titanic marked a harrowing bankruptcy within the deliver's records. The options made, the heroism displayed, and the tragedy that unfolds out within the icy waters of the North Atlantic live a poignant and enduring part of the deliver's legacy.

Investigations and Inquiries

In the aftermath of the Titanic disaster, a profound feel of surprise and grief reverberated round the area. This chapter delves into the great investigations and inquiries that followed the sinking of the Titanic, aiming to get to the lowest of the conditions and elements that added about the disaster.

A World in Mourning

The records of the Titanic's sinking sent shockwaves during the globe. The scale of the tragedy, with over 1,500 lives misplaced, added approximately an outpouring of grief and sympathy. It became an event that touched humans from all walks of lifestyles and taken a collective sense of sorrow.

Inquiries and Investigations

As the arena mourned, questions about the disaster's motives and the reaction of the Titanic's organization and operators started out out to emerge. Governments on each sides of the Atlantic released investigations and questions to discover the fact.

One of the maximum super inquiries changed into the British Wreck Commissioner's inquiry, led by using the usage of Lord Mersey. It sought to decide the conditions surrounding the collision with the iceberg and the deliver's actions at some point of and after the coincidence. Witness recollections from survivors and group members were important in piecing collectively the activities of that fateful night time.

The U.S. Senate Inquiry

Meanwhile, within the United States, the U.S. Senate convened its very non-public inquiry. This inquiry, chaired via Senator William Alden Smith, focused on the movements of the supply's operator, the White Star Line, and the maritime tips in location at the time.

Lessons Learned

The inquiries brought on numerous key findings and guidelines. They observed deficiencies in lifeboat ability, institution preparedness, and safety guidelines for transatlantic liners. As a end result, significant modifications have been implemented to decorate maritime protection, along with an boom within the enormous sort of lifeboats required on ships, better communication and emergency schooling for crews, and the recognition quo of the International Ice Patrol to expose iceberg actions inside the North Atlantic.

The Legacy of the Inquiries

The investigations and inquiries into the Titanic disaster left an indelible mark on maritime safety suggestions. The schooling located out from this tragedy maintain to form safety protocols and strategies for passenger vessels and function had a protracted-lasting effect at the prevention of comparable catastrophes within the future.

This financial disaster not handiest sheds slight on the investigations and inquiries that discovered the sinking of the Titanic but additionally serves as a testomony to the strength of mind of governments and the global network to prevent any such tragedy from regular. The legacy of those inquiries is a testomony to the long-lasting effect of the Titanic catastrophe on maritime safety.

Titanic's Legacy: Lessons Learned

The sinking of the Titanic had a profound and lasting effect on maritime protection and the area's notion of passenger supply adventure. This bankruptcy delves into the long-lasting legacy of the Titanic catastrophe and the education determined out that maintain to form the industry to at the existing time.

Safety Reforms and Regulations

The Titanic catastrophe prompted big adjustments within the maritime agency. Safety rules have been overhauled to prevent a recurrence of such a tragedy. Some of the critical issue reforms covered:

Increased Lifeboat Capacity: The most visible exchange modified into the requirement for ships to keep sufficient lifeboats for all passengers and organization. This mandate sought to make sure that, within the event of an emergency, there may be enough lifestyles-saving device available for everyone on board.

Safety Drills: The want for regular protection drills and training for both passengers and institution have become a important exercising. These drills protected the proper use of life jackets and lifeboats, emergency verbal exchange techniques, and the importance of maintaining calm and orderly behavior in the path of emergencies.

Enhanced Navigation Protocols: Improved navigation tactics were set up to keep away from areas with diagnosed ice risks. The reputation quo of the International Ice Patrol and the sharing of ice information among ships at sea contributed to extra constant voyages.

A Shift in Passenger Travel

The Titanic disaster had a profound impact on how passengers seemed deliver tour. The belief of invincibility that had surrounded the Titanic changed into modified via manner of a heightened recognition of the capability risks. Safety have become a paramount scenario for passengers and operators alike.

Many tourists decided on opportunity way of crossing the Atlantic, along with air journey, as they perceived it to be greater steady. Passenger ships have been not seen as unsinkable palaces but as vessels difficulty to the same vulnerabilities as some other mode of transportation.

Chapter 15: The Search For Titanic

The tale of the Titanic extends far beyond the supply's ill-fated voyage. It includes the first-rate journey to locate, find out, and file the final resting vicinity of the iconic vessel. This bankruptcy delves into the statistics of the search for the Titanic and the discoveries made during its exploration.

The Quest Begins

After the Titanic sank in 1912, its real place remained a mystery for many years. The deliver had long past down in the North Atlantic, a great and often treacherous expanse of ocean. The loss of specific coordinates and the regulations of generation on the time made the search for the Titanic a sincerely tough undertaking.

Breakthrough Discovery

In September 1985, the thriller turn out to be finally unraveled. Oceanographer Robert Ballard and a Franco-American day ride discovered the wreckage of the Titanic, mendacity and a 1/2 miles below the ground of the sea. The momentous discovery introduced the Titanic returned into the arena's highlight and opened the door to a new technology of exploration.

The wreckage became discovered scattered for the duration of the ocean ground, with the deliver's bow and stern separated thru a first-rate distance. The state of affairs of the ship, preserved by means of the bloodless depths and absence of natural slight, allowed for the recuperation of a wealth of records and artifacts.

Exploring the Underwater Museum

The exploration of the Titanic's stays has yielded an remarkable series of pictures, motion photographs, and three-D maps, providing an extensive have a look at the deliver's final resting place. Dives to the internet site have discovered out the supply's u . S . A . Of protection, further to the devices left behind via passengers and group.

The Titanic's iconic grand staircase, complicated woodwork, and factors of its opulent interior had been documented, permitting the arena to see the deliver as it existed in its heyday. The exploration has moreover supplied insights into the events important as a good buy due to the fact the disaster, which include the vicinity of the ship's impact with the iceberg.

Challenges of Preservation

The protection of the Titanic's remains has been a topic of debate and situation. The exploration of the internet site on-line has added about a extra know-how of the environmental effect at the supply, which includes the consequences of bacteria and salt corrosion. Balancing the selection to have a examine the deliver with the need to guard and maintain its stays has been an ongoing task.

The Titanic's Enduring Legacy

The discovery and exploration of the Titanic have completed a pivotal characteristic in maintaining the reminiscence of the supply alive. It has enabled the world to glimpse the beyond and advantage a deeper appreciation of the supply's grandeur and statistics. The artifacts recovered from the wreckage have been displayed in museums and exhibitions, allowing the general public to connect with the Titanic's story.

As we bypass forward in our exploration of the Titanic, we are able to keep to locate the mysteries and fascinating info surrounding this iconic vessel. The exploration of the Titanic's very last resting place remains an ongoing adventure, one which continues to shed mild on the iconic legacy of the supply and its vicinity in facts.

Titanic in Popular Culture

The story of the Titanic has transcended the geographical regions of history and tragedy to come to be a long-lasting part of well-known culture. This monetary ruin explores how the

Titanic has captured the world's creativeness and left an indelible mark on literature, film, art work, and track.

Literary Works

The Titanic's sinking has inspired infinite authors to pen novels, quick recollections, and non-fiction books. One of the earliest and maximum famous debts is "A Night to Remember" with the resource of Walter Lord, posted in 1955. This meticulously researched ebook added the activities of that fateful night time time to existence and served because the concept for plenty next works.

The Titanic has moreover regarded in numerous fictional novels, with authors exploring exchange situations, together with the supply's survival. The catastrophe has been a backdrop for memories of love, tragedy, and the human spirit.

Cinematic Legacy

The Titanic's tale has been immortalized on the silver display in numerous movies. The

1958 British film "A Night to Remember" emerge as one of the earliest cinematic variations of the catastrophe, closely following the sports activities as described in Walter Lord's book.

However, it turn out to be James Cameron's 1997 film, "Titanic," that catapulted the supply's story to a today's level of global recognition. Starring Leonardo DiCaprio and Kate Winslet, the film have come to be a cultural phenomenon, combining a love story with the historical tragedy. "Titanic" acquired 11 Academy Awards, along with Best Picture, and have emerge as the first-rate-grossing movie of its time.

Art and Music

The Titanic's story has been a supply of notion for artists and musicians. Painters have captured the deliver's grandeur, its final moments, and the aftermath of the disaster of their works. The supply's sinking has additionally been the difficulty of countless musical compositions, from classical quantities to famous songs.

The sinking of the Titanic is a everyday trouble remember in folks songs, presenting a medium for storytelling and remembrance. These songs often seize the emotions, tales, and legends that have advanced at some point of the deliver's fate.

The Enduring Fascination

The Titanic's enduring fascination in famous way of lifestyles is a testomony to its ability to move past time and connect with humans on a deeply emotional degree. Whether in books, films, artwork, or track, the deliver's story keeps to captivate new generations and serves as a reminder of the human potential for desire, heroism, and tragedy.

As we delve deeper into this financial ruin and discover the severa techniques the Titanic has motivated well-known culture, we're capable of benefit a more information of approaches this iconic vessel has left an indelible mark on the location's collective creativeness.

Titanic and Museums

The Titanic's legacy has been preserved and shared with the arena through the set up order of museums dedicated to the deliver's history. This financial ruin delves into the function of museums in commemorating the Titanic, keeping artifacts, and instructing the public about this iconic vessel and its tragic voyage.

The Birth of Titanic Museums

The first Titanic museum opened its doorways in 1987 in Halifax, Nova Scotia, a city carefully related to the disaster due to its feature in the recovery of the Titanic's sufferers. The museum's collection includes artifacts, non-public gadgets, and historic files associated with the ship and its passengers.

Titanic Belfast

One of the most renowned Titanic museums is Titanic Belfast, positioned within the metropolis wherein the ship end up constructed. Opened in 2012, this museum is housed in a putting constructing that resembles the supply's prow. It offers a comprehensive and immersive enjoy, with interactive well-knownshows, replicas of supply interiors, and an extensive exploration of Belfast's shipbuilding ancient past.

Artifact Exhibitions

Titanic museums round the area regularly characteristic exhibitions of artifacts recovered from the deliver's wreckage. These objects, which incorporates rings, clothing, dinnerware, and private property, provide a tangible connection to the beyond and provide web page visitors a glimpse into the lives of these on board.

Education and Commemoration

Titanic museums characteristic educational hubs, imparting belief into the deliver's records, the activities fundamental to the catastrophe, and the training determined. They offer packages, workshops, and lectures for university college students and site visitors of every age, fostering an know-how of the Titanic's enduring legacy.

Remembering the Lives Lost

Museums additionally play a critical position in commemorating the lives misplaced in the Titanic catastrophe. They often maintain memorials and honor boards that pay tribute to the passengers and crew who perished. These memorials function a poignant reminder of the human charge of the tragedy.

The Future of Titanic Museums

The importance of Titanic museums in retaining and sharing the deliver's records with destiny generations can not be overstated. As technology advances, museums are more and more the usage of virtual truth, augmented fact, and virtual statistics to decorate the visitor experience and make certain that the memory of the Titanic endures.

As we preserve to find out the location of Titanic museums in commemorating the ship and its legacy, we gain a deeper appreciation for the efforts to hold the tale of the Titanic alive and to honor the lives misplaced on that fateful night time time in April 1912.

Chapter 16: Titanic's Enduring Mysteries

Despite a few years of research and exploration, the Titanic continues to preserve its share of mysteries and unanswered questions. This bankruptcy delves into a number of the long-lasting enigmas and puzzles surrounding the supply, its passengers, and the occasions of that fateful night time.

The Mystery of the Whistle

One of the enduring questions related to the Titanic centers on the supply's whistle. Many bills from the disaster point out the haunting sound of the ship's whistle blowing as it sank. However, it remains uncertain whether or not or now not the deliver's engineers or every different crewmember become chargeable for sounding the whistle because the Titanic went down.

The Mystery of the Binoculars

Another unsolved thriller is the absence of binoculars inside the crow's nest, the lookout function inside the supply's crow's nest. Binoculars can also additionally want to have carried out a crucial feature in spotting the iceberg earlier and retaining off the collision. To at the prevailing time, it is dubious why binoculars had been no longer available to the lookouts.

The Mystery of the Submersibles

Submersible exploration of the Titanic has yielded a wealth of data, but it has furthermore left at the back of many unanswered questions. The excessive strain and severe conditions at the sea ground have made it hard to retrieve effective artifacts and portions of the supply, leaving additives of the Titanic despite the fact that shrouded in thriller.

The Mystery of the California

The deliver Californian, which turn out to be within the vicinity of the Titanic at the night time time of the catastrophe, has been a subject of controversy. The Californian modified into interior visible sort of the sinking supply but did not reply to its distress indicators promptly. Questions surrounding the Californian's actions, or lack thereof, persist.

The Mystery of Passengers and Crew

Individual recollections of passengers and group who have been on board the Titanic on that fateful night time time time keep to captivate historians and researchers. While many debts were documented, there are even though gaps in our know-how approximately the research, moves, and alternatives made with the useful resource of folks who have been aboard the deliver.

The Unanswered Questions

The Titanic's enduring mysteries remind us that, in spite of our great efforts to locate the fact, some factors of the disaster also can additionally in no way be completely defined. These unanswered questions upload to the intrigue and complexity of the Titanic's story, keeping the world's fascination alive.

As we delve further into this monetary spoil, we're able to discover some of those enduring mysteries in extra detail, losing mild on the persevering with efforts to remedy the enigmas that keep shrouding the Titanic's history.

Titanic: Remembering and Honoring

The tale of the Titanic isn't always quality a tale of tragedy and thriller; it's also a tale of remembrance and commemoration. This financial ruin focuses on the various techniques in which the Titanic is remembered and honored, from annual ceremonies to innovative expressions that pay tribute to the deliver and its passengers.

Annual Memorial Services

Throughout the area, annual memorial services are held to recollect the lives misplaced within the Titanic disaster. These services frequently take region on or round

April fifteenth, the anniversary of the ship's sinking. They function a solemn reminder of the human toll of the tragedy and provide an possibility for reflected image and remembrance.

Memorial Sites

There are severa bodily web sites that characteristic memorials to the Titanic and its passengers. Halifax, Nova Scotia, domestic to the severa Titanic's sufferers who've been recovered from the sea, has numerous monuments and cemeteries devoted to the deliver's memory. These internet websites permit visitors to pay their respects to the souls out of place in the catastrophe.

Artistic Tributes

Artists from numerous disciplines have used their talents to pay tribute to the Titanic. Painters, sculptors, musicians, and writers have created works that seize the supply's grandeur and the emotions surrounding its sinking. These imaginitive expressions characteristic a way of honoring the Titanic's legacy.

Documentary Films

Documentary films have carried out a massive position in commemorating the Titanic and educating the general public approximately the catastrophe. These movies regularly combine archival photos, interviews with survivors or their descendants, and professional assessment to provide a whole information of the deliver's data and the events of that night time.

Continuing Research

Researchers, historians, and explorers maintain to make a contribution to the continuing commemoration of the Titanic. Their paintings in uncovering new records, answering lengthy-popularity questions, and preserving the supply's information ensures that the legacy of the Titanic stays colorful and applicable.

The Immortal Ship

The Titanic's enduring place in our collective reminiscence reminds us of the effect of the disaster on the area. It serves as a image of the human functionality for choice and heroism, even in the face of overwhelming tragedy. The deliver's story maintains to resonate with human beings of each age, and its legacy lives on in numerous forms.

In this bankruptcy, we are able to discover the various approaches in which the Titanic is remembered and venerated. From annual rituals to creative expressions, the iconic fascination with the Titanic is a testament to the iconic effect of this ancient occasion.

The Titanic's Timeless Lessons

The Titanic's legacy is greater than handiest a ancient account of a disaster; it imparts timeless schooling that preserve to resonate with human beings across the area. In this very last financial catastrophe, we reflect on the long-lasting records that the Titanic has to offer.

The Hubris of Overconfidence

The notion in the Titanic's unsinkability serves as a stark reminder of the dangers of overconfidence. The ship's tragic future teaches us that no matter how advanced or stable we can also sense, we need to remain vigilant and prepared for sudden disturbing conditions.

The Human Spirit in Times of Crisis

The Titanic disaster showcases the amazing resilience of the human spirit. Acts of heroism and sacrifice had been ample, as passengers and company positioned the welfare of others earlier than their very personal. The supply's story exemplifies the electricity of the human man or woman inside the face of adversity.

The Importance of Preparedness

The Titanic's loss of adequate lifeboats and the crew's unfamiliarity with emergency strategies underscore the important significance of preparedness. The disaster compels us to make sure that we are organized to reply to surprising crises, whether or not at sea or in our regular lives.

The Price of Inaction

The failure of the close by deliver Californian to reply right away to the Titanic's distress signs reminds us of the effects of inaction in instances of disaster. The Californian's now not on time reaction serves as a poignant lesson in the importance of taking decisive and well timed motion to useful resource those in want.

A Legacy of Remembrance

The Titanic's tale is a reminder of the power of remembrance. Memorials, museums, and annual ceremonies serve as a testament to the long-lasting importance of the deliver's facts. They make sure that the lives out of place within the disaster aren't forgotten and that the instructions found out are exceeded down thru the generations.

The Titanic's Legacy

As we end our exploration of the Titanic's story, we are left with a profound appreciation for the supply's enduring legacy. The instructions of the Titanic cross beyond time and hold to guide us in our quest for protection, preparedness, and the renovation of the human spirit.

The Titanic's tale remains a poignant and compelling narrative on the way to keep captivating and educating folks who are looking for to apprehend the sports of that fateful night time in April 1912. It stands as a testament to the indomitable spirit of humanity within the face of the best challenges and reminds us of the enduring electricity of remembrance and commands determined out.

Chapter 17: Birth Of The Legend

In the tumultuous beginning a few years of the 20 th century, an age of relentless improvement and unequalled ambition, a legend end up quietly taking form. The saga of the Titanic began now not with the pounding of rivets or the roar of engines but in the minds of fellows who dared to dream on a large scale.

The start of this legend has grow to be a tale etched in ambition and advised with the aid of an audacious imaginative and prescient. To understand its genesis, one ought to venture again to a time whilst the area become intoxicated with dreams of conquest—the conquest of the land, the sky, and, maximum daringly, the sea's depths.

At the helm of this grand project changed into the White Star Line, a excellent pressure in transatlantic excursion. For them, the Titanic have turn out to be to be extra than simply every different addition to their illustrious fleet. She have grow to be to be a statement, a surprise that would go away an indelible imprint at the area.

The White Star Line's dealing with director, Bruce Is might also additionally, changed into a man ate up thru grandeur. He noticed the Titanic no longer definitely as a vessel but as a vessel of goals. With a crew of gifted engineers and naval architects, he got all the way down to conceive a deliver that would bypass past all that had come earlier than it.

The name Titanic modified into carefully selected, evoking an photo of tremendous strength and immensity. But it changed into no longer sincerely in the phrase that this deliver modified into destined for greatness however in her layout, introduction, and destiny.

The perplexity of this assignment lay now not surely in her size but in her idea. The designers sought to create a floating paradise, a international of luxurious catering to the whims and desires of the maximum discerning passengers. She come to be a testomony to the capability of technology and human ingenuity, and her very life modified into to be an embodiment of an era characterized thru way of rapid industrialization and unyielding improvement.

The plans for the Titanic had been an complex mixture of architectural brilliance and engineering prowess. Her strains had been to be smooth, her grandeur top notch, and her capacity for passengers and load remarkable. She grow to be to be a surprise of modernity, seamlessly melding the classical splendor of the Ritz and the Louvre with the modern-day innovation of the age.

As the vision took shape on paper, the area watched in anticipation. The significance of the Titanic's project modified into no longer out of place on everybody. Newspapers regaled their readers with memories of her coming close to near splendor. Passengers eager for a taste of costly clamored for tickets. And within the shipyards, a hive of hobby resonated with the symphony of advent. The worldwide had turn out to be a theater, with the Titanic as its celeb, and he or she have become poised to take middle diploma.

In Belfast, Ireland, a city teeming with enterprise, the begin of the Titanic have turn out to be no ordinary affair. Over 3 thousand skilled human beings had been summoned to mold her into fact. The approach turn out to be a surprise of human coordination and craftsmanship, wherein the artistry of metal, the precision of rivets, and the labor of infinite fingers blended to shape an icon.

Yet, what definitely set the Titanic apart changed into the unwavering conviction that she modified into impervious to the perils of the ocean. This belief in her 'unsinkable' nature have become now not mere marketing and advertising hyperbole but a tenet upon which her very layout changed into predicated. The Titanic had superior protection talents, which includes a double hull and watertight cubicles designed to thwart disaster.

In the very last ranges of her start, the sector held its breath. The Titanic manifested human ambition, symbolizing a society that had come of age in an generation of technological marvels and global exploration. She embodied an epoch that had staked its declare to the destiny with unshakable self perception.

As we traverse thru the convoluted corridors of this biography, we are able to maintain to navigate the perplexity and burstiness of this epochal tale. In all its unique beauty, this financial damage is the prologue to a story that encompasses human ambition, ingenuity, and, in the end, a future no person ought to have foreseen. The Titanic changed into greater than a deliver; it manifested the human spirit's ceaseless pressure to overcome the elements and declare dominion over the unpredictable and unforgiving sea. And, as she changed into poised to embark on her maiden voyage, the arena held its breath, unknowing of the dramatic future that lay ahead, for the legend had only without a doubt begun to take shape.

The Genesis of Titanic

In the annals of records, Titanic has come to be synonymous with grandeur, tragedy, and an indomitable spirit of innovation. Her tale isn't without a doubt one among a supply by myself but a voyage into the coronary coronary heart of an technology, an epoch marked by way of the use of improvement, ambition, and a persevering with choice to conquer the unknown. To surely fathom the essence of the Titanic, one want to journey another time to the tumultuous times in which she was conceived – an age even as humanity's insatiable thirst for progress set the volume for the shipping of a legend.

At the helm of this audacious project stood the White Star Line, renowned for its transatlantic prowess. However, their vision extended a protracted manner past the horizon; it reached for the celebs. Their aspiration modified into encapsulated inside the grandeur of the Titanic. This vessel emerge as not merely to move passengers throughout the ocean however to transport them right into a cutting-edge realm of high priced and safety.

In the person of Bruce Ismay, the White Star Line located a charismatic chief whose ambition knew no bounds. He viewed the Titanic as not an insignificant deliver however a microcosm of society's most aspirations. Ismay's vision became unwavering, his strength of mind resolute. He noticed the Titanic as a vessel of goals and became determined to convey the ones desires to existence.

The name "Titanic" come to be cautiously selected, evoking an image of big strength and grandiosity. This emerge as not an arbitrary choice but a assertion, a harbinger of a legend. The name conveyed a enjoy of immensity, of a deliver that might dwarf all others.

What set the Titanic apart from her contemporaries was her ambition. This modified into not a vessel supposed for mere transportation; she have become designed to be a floating paradise. Her creators, a team of proficient engineers, naval architects, and designers, sought to marry the aesthetics of classical highly-priced with the modern-day innovations of the age. The Titanic become to be a masterpiece, a testomony to the ability of era and human imagination.

As the plans for the Titanic took form on paper, the arena watched with bated breath. Newspapers carried reminiscences of her drawing close grandeur, passengers clamored for tickets, and shipyards buzzed with anticipation. The global grow to be a diploma, and the Titanic become to be its famous individual. It become a period marked with the resource of a burst of hobby and corporation, in which perplexity have become met with the audacity of human ambition.

In the shipyards of Belfast, Ireland, over three thousand skilled craftsmen labored relentlessly. The advent of the Titanic grow to be no longer an insignificant undertaking; it changed proper into a spectacle, a symphony of steel and rivets that gave shipping to a vessel the sector had in no way seen earlier than. She manifested human coordination, craftsmanship, and the wedding of artistry and engineering.

However, what truely defined the Titanic turn out to be the unshakable perception in her 'unsinkable' nature. This emerge as no longer a trifling advertising and marketing and marketing gimmick however a essential tenet upon which her layout have become predicated. The Titanic had innovative superior safety features, which incorporates a double hull and watertight booths. She modified into designed to thwart disaster, to defy the very elements that had claimed such loads of ships earlier than her.

As the Titanic neared final touch, she become extra than most effective a deliver. She modified proper right into a photograph of an era, an brand of a society that had come of age in a time of technological marvels and international exploration. She embodied an epoch that had staked its claim to the future with unyielding self assurance.

In the chapters to come lower back, we are able to delve deeper into the coronary heart of this excellent story. We will discover the men and women who conceived and crafted the Titanic, individuals who breathed lifestyles into her, and those who launched into a adventure that would all of the time be etched in the annals of facts.

The shipping of the Titanic modified into more than a production mission; it became the culmination of a dream that had captured the arena's imagination. It modified into a 2d in facts while technology, ambition, and aspiration converged, giving delivery to a deliver that symbolized an age characterised thru audacity and opulence.

The Titanic have become now not only a deliver in a worldwide marked by manner of using development and ambition. She come to be a testomony to the ceaseless human strain to triumph over the elements and claim dominion over the unpredictable and unforgiving sea. As she have end up poised to embark on her maiden voyage, the area held its collective breath, unknowing of the dramatic future earlier, for the legend had handiest honestly commenced to take shape.

Visionaries Behind the Dream: Crafting the Titanic's Ambition

The Titanic is an prolonged lasting testomony to conceitedness and ambition inside the storied annals of human success. She was no ordinary ship; she have come to be a manifestation of the grand desires and constant spirit of innovation that described the early twentieth century. But in the decrease returned of the breathtaking scale and luxury of the Titanic's creation had been the visionaries who dared to dream on a scale that would captivate the arena.

The heartbeat of this dream emanated from the hallowed halls of the White Star Line, a call that carried massive weight inside the realm of transatlantic journey. Their imaginative and prescient, but, reached a ways past the shores and horizons; it went for the very stars. The Titanic have grow to be no longer merely a supply however a voyage into the coronary coronary heart of society's most aspirations.

At the helm of this audacious assignment modified into someone whose name should come to be synonymous with the Titanic's inception: Bruce Ismay. As the coping with director of the White Star Line, Ismay become a charismatic leader whose ambition knew no bounds. He saw the Titanic as a vessel and a deliver of goals. His vision became dependable, his dedication unyielding. Ismay believed that the Titanic may additionally additionally need to redefine luxurious excursion and end up determined in making that belief a reality.

The call "Titanic" come to be carefully selected, resonating with an air of mystery of big electricity and grandiosity. This turn out to be now not mere terminology however a declaration, a precursor of the legend taking form. The name conveyed a experience of immensity, of a supply that might dwarf all that had come earlier than it.

The dream changed into now not without a doubt approximately nomenclature however the layout, manufacturing, and final adventure. A exquisite group of engineers, naval architects, and architects labored tirelessly to respire life into the Titanic's blueprint. Their task modified into large; they sought to fuse classical beauty with cutting-edge innovation. The Titanic modified into to be a masterpiece, a work of art and generation that might all of the time redefine the opportunities of marine engineering.

As the Titanic's layout took form on paper, the area watched with awe and anticipation. Newspapers chronicled her drawing close grandeur, passengers vied to experience her pricey, and shipyards teemed with hobby. The worldwide modified into converted proper right right into a degree, with the Titanic as its big name. This length changed into marked thru an terrific burst of motion, an age of development that met the perplexity of the unknown with an audacity that could all the time etch the Titanic into records.

More than 3 thousand expert craftsmen worked regularly inside the shipyards of Belfast, Ireland, wherein she took her tangible form. The manufacturing of the Titanic became no regular challenge; it modified into an first rate spectacle. It end up a symphony of metal and rivets, wherein artistry and engineering combined to shape a vessel the likes of which the sector had by no means seen. The Titanic became a marvel of human coordination and craftsmanship, a testament to the audacity and innovation of the age.

Yet, what definitely set the Titanic apart have become her 'unsinkable' nature. This changed into no longer mere rhetoric however a middle principle upon which her layout have become grounded. The Titanic became fortified with superior protection functions, along with a double hull and watertight cubicles, which have been taken into consideration groundbreaking for his or her time. She become engineered to defy disaster, to transcend the maritime tragedies of the beyond.

As the Titanic neared completion, she became not only a supply but a picture of an generation, an emblem of a society that had come of age in an epoch marked through technological marvels and international exploration. She embodied a time that had staked its declare to the future with unwavering self notion. The Titanic modified into a vessel of goals that might sail the seas of human ambition.

In the chapters, we are able to delve deeper into the coronary coronary coronary heart of this exquisite story. We will discover the lives of individuals who conceived and crafted the Titanic, folks who breathed life into her, and those who released into a adventure that would end up etched in the annals of statistics.

The transport of the Titanic changed into more than absolutely the improvement of a ship; it turned into the fruits of a dream that had captured the sector's imagination. It changed into a 2d in statistics while generation, ambition, and aspiration converged, giving start to a vessel that could all the time be a image of an age characterized by using using audacity and opulence.

The Titanic have grow to be no longer handiest a deliver in a international marked by way of using development and ambition.

She turn out to be a testomony to the ceaseless human pressure to conquer the factors and lay claim to the unpredictable and unforgiving sea. As she stood poised for her maiden voyage, the place held its collective breath, unknowing of the dramatic future that awaited her—for the legend of the Titanic had nice surely began to take form.

Chapter 18: Design And Construction

In the coronary coronary heart of Belfast, in opposition to an enterprise revolution that had changed the arena, the Titanic end up emerging as a testament to human audacity and ingenuity. The White Star Line's imaginative and prescient for the Titanic become not something short of awe-inspiring; it become a feat of engineering and format that would move past the bounds of what have become deemed viable.

Creating this unsinkable legend have become no longer a easy assignment; it grow to be a complex ballet of creativity and engineering. It have turn out to be an business enterprise marked via perplexity and burstiness, a whirlwind of ambition that sought to bridge the chasm between goals and reality. The Titanic turned into no longer in fact a vessel but an embodiment of an generation marked by means of using the use of fast industrialization and relentless development.

The Titanic's architects and engineers had been not content cloth with building a supply. They aimed to craft a vessel that would redefine luxurious at sea and the arena at large. Their perception was drawn from the maximum expensive structures of the time, incorporating the classical splendor of the Ritz and the Louvre, all at the equal time as embracing the present day-day upgrades of present day engineering.

The stop end result become a ship that changed into, without exaggeration, peerless in its grandeur. The Titanic come to be to be a masterpiece of layout, an steeply-priced surprise that would enchant passengers from all walks of lifestyles. The superb cabins had been to be replete with silk sheets, top notch china, and the fine offerings. At the equal time, the 1/three-elegance quarters, even though a bargain an awful lot less big, were but a much cry from the hardships that passengers typically skilled on transatlantic voyages.

Beyond aesthetics, the Titanic grow to be designed with protection as a paramount concern. The specter of previous maritime disasters loomed large, and the supply's creators have been determined to spare no price in ensuring the safety of passengers and team. The double hull and watertight cubicles were pioneering protection capabilities designed to hold the deliver afloat even in a collision. It changed right into a testament to the meticulous making plans that went into her creation.

As the plans for the Titanic took form, the arena watched with bated breath. Newspapers carried recollections of her drawing near grandeur, passengers vied to experience her high priced, and shipyards thrummed with palpable anticipation. The international had end up a level, with the Titanic as its famous person, and she or he or he modified into poised to take center degree.

The manufacturing of the Titanic became no longer only a bodily business enterprise; it changed proper into a manifestation of the dream that had captured the area's imagination. In the shipyards of Belfast, greater than three thousand skilled craftsmen worked tirelessly to form her into reality. It changed into a symphony of coordination, craftsmanship, and the wedding of artistry and engineering.

Yet, what clearly set the Titanic apart emerge as the unyielding notion in her 'unsinkable' nature. This conviction emerge as not mere advertising and marketing hyperbole however a center precept upon which her design have become predicated. The Titanic have become fortified with advanced protection features taken into consideration groundbreaking for the time. It grow to be a vessel engineered to go beyond the maritime tragedies of the past.

In the very last tiers of her delivery, the area held its breath. The Titanic turned into more than high-quality a supply; it symbolized an era, an logo of a society that had come of age in a time of technological marvels and international exploration. She embodied an epoch that had staked its claim to the future with unwavering self belief.

In the chapters, we are able to delve deeper into the coronary heart of this fantastic tale. We will uncover the lives of folks that conceived and crafted the Titanic, people who breathed lifestyles into her, and those who released into a journey that could grow to be etched in the annals of history.

The design and production of the Titanic had been no longer mere engineering feats; they were a testomony to the boundless human spirit, to the ceaseless pursuit of development and innovation. The Titanic changed into greater than a supply; she embodied an era of audacity and opulence. As she stood poised for her maiden voyage, the world held its collective breath, unknowing of the dramatic destiny that awaited her—for the legend of the Titanic had only clearly all commenced to take shape.

Building the "Unsinkable" Ship

The dream of the Titanic turned into taking shape inside the sprawling shipyards of Belfast amidst the clanging of metallic and the symphony of hard paintings. This dream defied conventions and driven the limits of human ambition. The White Star Line, a industrial business enterprise agency that had earned its recognition for luxurious transatlantic excursion, had set its attractions on crafting a vessel that would now not just outshine the competition but pass beyond the very notion of maritime opulence.

At the helm of this audacious challenge have turn out to be Bruce Ismay, the dynamic coping with director of the White Star Line. He changed into a person possessed through grandeur who saw the Titanic no longer as a supply however as a floating palace, a shifting artwork of paintings, and an embodiment of human improvement. His vision come to be unshakable, his determination unyielding. To Ismay, the Titanic modified into no longer surely a vessel but a vessel of desires.

The name "Titanic" changed into now not decided on arbitrarily. It have become a deliberate preference meant to evoke an photo of significant electricity and grandiosity. The call itself carried a feel of immensity, of a supply that would dwarf all others. The Titanic changed into to be extra than a deliver; she come to be a legend.

The creators of the Titanic did now not intention for mediocrity; they sought to redefine luxury. The deliver's layout became a wedding of classical splendor and modern innovation. Her strains had been to be each sleek and enforcing, a harmonious mixture of shape and feature. In the complicated blueprint of the Titanic, perplexity and innovation merged, giving starting to a deliver of first-rate scale and ambition.

The international watched with bated breath because the Titanic's format took shape on paper. Newspapers regaled their readers with testimonies of her coming near near beauty, passengers vied to enjoy her pricey, and the shipyards resounded with an almost palpable experience of anticipation. The international had emerge as a degree, and the Titanic changed into to be its famous individual. It became a time marked with the aid of manner of a burst of hobby and employer at the identical time as human ambition met the perplexity of the unknown with unwavering audacity.

The manufacturing of the Titanic changed into no normal feat. Over 3 thousand professional craftsmen toiled relentlessly within the shipyards of Belfast, Ireland. The method modified into more than only a bodily endeavor; it turned into a surprise of human coordination and craftsmanship. It become a symphony of metal and rivets, wherein artistry and engineering melded to create a vessel that stood as an icon of an age bursting with development and innovation.

What in truth set the Titanic aside was the unwavering belief in her 'unsinkable' nature. This grow to be not a mere advertising and marketing slogan however a essential precept upon which her layout have come to be built. The Titanic had groundbreaking superior protection capabilities, which consist of a double hull and watertight booths. She modified into designed to thwart catastrophe, to defy the very factors that had claimed such some of ships before her.

In the final ranges of her creation, the arena held its breath. The Titanic emerge as not only a ship; she embodied an generation marked via audacity and comfort, an era that had come of age in a time of technological marvels and worldwide exploration. She symbolized an epoch that had staked its declare to the destiny with unshakable self belief.

As we traverse thru the tricky narrative of this biography, we are able to hold to navigate the perplexity and burstiness of this epochal tale.

The building of the Titanic grow to be now not best a production venture; it turn out to be the culmination of a dream that had captured the area's imagination. It come to be a second in statistics when generation, ambition, and aspiration converged, giving delivery to a vessel that might all of the time be a image of an age characterised thru audacity and opulence.

The Titanic turn out to be not simplest a deliver in a global marked thru development and ambition. She become a testament to the ceaseless human energy to overcome the elements and lay declare to the unpredictable and unforgiving sea. As she stood poised for her maiden voyage, the arena held its collective breath, unknowing of the dramatic destiny that awaited her—for the legend of the Titanic had only without a doubt began out to take shape.

Technological Marvels of Her Time

The Titanic changed into no longer just a deliver; she come to be a living testomony to an age that had launched into an unrelenting quest to triumph over the world's mightiest adversary—the unpredictable and unforgiving sea. Progress turned into the clarion name within the early twentieth century, and the arena changed into amid a technological revolution that defied imagination. The Titanic become to be more than a vessel; she symbolized the epoch's boundless ambition, a fusion of synthetic marvels, and a declaration of human mastery over the factors.

The White Star Line, a corporation with a storied history in transatlantic excursion, have become at the helm of this organization. They had set their attractions on growing a deliver that could no longer simply sail sooner or later of the sea but redefine pricey and opulence. The driving pressure in the back of this ambition become Bruce Ismay, the managing director of the White Star Line. To him, the Titanic grow to be more than most effective a deliver; she have become a vision of desires found out. Ismay's unwavering conviction have become that the Titanic may need to head past all that had come in advance than, and he became decided to make that conviction a truth.

The very call "Titanic" changed into cautiously determined on. It evoked a experience of huge electricity and grandiosity, a name that symbolized the audacity of the age. But it wasn't handiest in name that this deliver modified into formidable; it modified into in her layout and creation.

The Titanic's architects and engineers sought to marry the elegance of classical costly with the cutting-edge enhancements of the generation. The deliver have become to be a masterpiece, an embodiment of the functionality of era and human creativeness. Her format combined grace and functionality, a harmonious fusion that left the place in awe.

The worldwide watched with marvel and anticipation because the Titanic's blueprints started out forming. Newspapers were full of tales of her impending beauty, passengers had been eager to stable passage on her maiden voyage, and the shipyards echoed with the hum of hobby. The global had end up a level, with the Titanic as its superstar. This turn out to be an age marked through the usage of a burst of motion while human ambition met the perplexity of the unknown with unwavering audacity.

The production of the Titanic grow to be no longer only a physical task; it changed right into a testament to human coordination, craftsmanship, and the seamless marriage of artistry and engineering. In the shipyards of Belfast, Ireland, over three thousand expert craftsmen worked relentlessly to supply her into lifestyles. The manner grow to be more than handiest a introduction task; it became a symphony of steel and rivets, in which artistry and engineering combined to shape an icon.

Yet what surely set the Titanic aside emerge as the belief in her 'unsinkable' nature. It modified into not only a marketing slogan; it changed into a middle tenet upon which her layout have become built. The Titanic had contemporary superior safety skills, such as a double hull and watertight cubicles. She became engineered to face as much as the unpredictable factors of the sea, designed to defy disaster.

In the very last ranges of her production, the arena held its breath. The Titanic modified into no longer just a deliver; it become a photograph of an generation marked thru audacity and comfort, an era that had come of age in a time of technological marvels and international exploration. She embodied an epoch that had staked its claim to the future with unshakable self guarantee.

As we journey through the complexities of this biography, we maintain to find out the perplexity and burstiness of an generation that birthed the Titanic. Her introduction modified into now not simply an engineering wonder; it modified proper into a manifestation of human ambition, innovation, and an unwavering belief in the strength of improvement.

The Titanic modified into now not handiest a deliver in a international marked via way of progress and ambition. She symbolized the ceaseless human stress to overcome the elements and stake a declare over the unpredictable and unforgiving sea. As she prepared to sail on her maiden voyage, the arena held its breath, unaware of the dramatic future that awaited her—for the legend of the Titanic had handiest just all commenced to take form.

Chapter 19: Maiden Voyage

As the Titanic stood resplendent on the dock in Southampton, her name already a byword for high priced and grandeur, the arena held its breath. This have come to be not only a supply putting sail; it have turn out to be a second in information, a fruits of dreams and objectives woven collectively in an audacious tapestry. The Titanic grow to be no longer most effective a vessel; she have emerge as an icon of an technology that had ventured to conquer the elements, an embodiment of the relentless spirit of innovation that defined the early 20th century.

Her departure modified proper right into a spectacle that defied the creativeness. A cacophony of cheers and applause crammed the air as passengers, from the maximum illustrious to the maximum humble, streamed on board. It turn out to be a circulate-section of society, a dwelling testomony to the Titanic's enchantment.

The tremendous passengers reveled within the splendor that surrounded them. Their cabins had been a haven of luxury, with plush carpets, silk sheets, and the best facilities. They dined on expensive food served in gilded ingesting rooms, wherein the air come to be thick with the promise of grandeur. The Titanic have come to be a supply designed to move them proper proper right into a international of extravagance, and it did so with aplomb.

But the Titanic changed into more than really wonderful opulence. In the zero.33-elegance quarters, passengers who had never dreamed of this sort of adventure found themselves in a international of relative consolation. They had been far from the hardships that zero.33-elegance vacationers on specific ships commonly endured. The Titanic modified into, in her way, a vessel of desires for people who had released into her.

As the supply set sail, it wasn't simply her passengers who marveled at her grandeur;

the arena watched in awe. Newspapers carried recollections of her splendor, and the concept of the 'unsinkable' supply had captured the public's imagination. The Titanic modified into greater than a vessel; it symbolized human ambition and innovation, a testomony to the ceaseless pursuit of improvement.

The voyage modified into marked with the resource of a experience of optimism, a belief that the location changed into at the cusp of a new era. It become a time at the same time as technology and ambition knew no bounds, and the Titanic epitomized that spirit. She embodied a society that had come of age in an epoch of technological marvels and international exploration. Her maiden voyage changed right into a journey into the heart of an technology that had staked its claim to the destiny with unshakable self assurance.

But the destiny held secrets and techniques and strategies that the Titanic could not fathom. She changed right into a marvel of engineering and layout however modified into not invincible. The sea, unforgiving and unpredictable, had dominion over all. As the Titanic launched into its maiden voyage, the arena grow to be ignorant of its dramatic destiny.

The voyage blended highly-priced and exhilaration, a microcosm of the area itself. First-class passengers reveled in the luxurious surrounding them, whilst 1/3-beauty tourists determined a diploma of consolation that that they had in no way imagined. The supply sailed thru calm waters with the promise of a vibrant destiny on the horizon.

Yet, it turn out to be a promise that might live unfulfilled. The Titanic's maiden voyage become destined to turn out to be a bankruptcy within the annals of records, a tale of ambition, expensive, and tragedy. The legend of the Titanic have emerge as not pretty much her production however her journey, which might all the time etch her call within the collective memory of humanity.

As we delve deeper into the chapters of this biography, we maintain to navigate the perplexity and burstiness of the Titanic's tale. Her maiden voyage turn out to be a adventure at some point of the sea and into the coronary coronary heart of an technology marked by way of audacity and opulence. And due to the truth the Titanic sailed onto the horizon, the world held its collective breath, unknowing of its dramatic destiny, for the legend had pleasant simply started out to take shape.

Eager Expectations

In the early hours of April 10, 1912, due to the fact the Titanic sat resplendent in Southampton's harbor, a palpable revel in of anticipation filled the crisp sea air. This became no longer clearly a deliver approximately to embark on a voyage; it symbolized an age marked by using manner of unparalleled ambition and unquenchable optimism. The Titanic emerge as no longer best a vessel; she embodied the desires and expectations of an entire epoch.

On the dock, a scene spread out that defied imagination. First-splendor passengers, embellished in their best apparel, stood with a feel of regal expectation. Their cabins, a haven of costly and opulence, awaited them with the promise of grandeur. The Titanic become more than only a deliver to them; it have become an extravagant experience, a voyage proper proper into a international of exceptional extravagance.

The enchantment of the Titanic become now not constrained to the privileged few in first beauty. In the 1/3-elegance quarters, passengers who had in no way dared dream of this sort of journey decided themselves in a international of relative consolation. The Titanic became, in its manner, a vessel of desires for folks that had launched into her. The adventure transcended beauty and history, a testament to the Titanic's conventional attraction.

As passengers streamed on board, they carried with them the desires and aspirations of a global on the brink of transformation. The Titanic have become not best a deliver putting sail; it have come to be a declaration of an generation that had launched into a quest to triumph over the elements, an embodiment of the relentless spirit of innovation that characterized the early twentieth century. Her departure changed into not most effective a voyage however a promise of improvement.

But the attraction of the Titanic became no longer restricted to her passengers and team. The international itself watched with a feel of awe and expectation. Newspapers carried recollections of her beauty, and the concept of the 'unsinkable' supply had captured the collective imagination. The Titanic end up now not handiest a vessel however a photo of human ambition and innovation, a testomony to the ceaseless pursuit of development.

The Titanic's maiden voyage have become marked by means of optimism and a belief that the arena emerge as at the precipice of a present day generation. It became an age even as era and ambition knew no bounds, and the Titanic epitomized that spirit. She embodied a society that had come of age in an epoch of technological marvels and international exploration. Her departure have come to be now not most effective a journey into the Atlantic but into the coronary heart of an generation that had staked its declare to the destiny with unwavering self assurance.

Yet, while the Titanic set sail, the ocean held secrets and techniques and techniques she couldn't fathom. She changed proper right into a marvel of engineering and format however have turn out to be now not invincible. The sea, unforgiving and unpredictable, had dominion over all. Her keen expectancies had been met with a future that might for all time etch her name inside the annals of records.

As we traverse the complex narrative of this biography, we hold to discover the perplexity and burstiness of the Titanic's tale. Her maiden voyage have become a adventure across the sea and into the coronary coronary heart of an technology marked through audacity and opulence. As the Titanic sailed into the horizon, the region held its breath, blind to its dramatic future. For the legend, it had high-quality simply commenced out to take form.

Setting Sail for History

As the clock arms pointed to midday on April 10, 1912, the sprawling metropolis of Southampton bore witness to an event that is probably etched into the annals of records. The White Star Line's crown jewel, the Titanic, stood organized to sail. She modified into not most effective a deliver; she emerge as the embodiment of human ambition, an audacious proclamation of the energy of improvement, and a photograph of a global getting ready to transformation.

The scenes on the Southampton dock defied imagination. First-elegance passengers, adorned in their maximum luxurious apparel, exuded an air of regal anticipation. For them, the Titanic changed into no longer best a supply; she became a promise of extremely good luxurious and opulence. The sumptuous cabins that awaited them held the attraction of grandeur and extravagance. This have become no longer an insignificant voyage but an immersion right into a worldwide of indulgence.

But the enchantment of the Titanic grow to be now not constrained to the elite. In the 1/3-beauty quarters, passengers who had handiest dared to dream of this type of journey determined themselves in a worldwide of relative comfort. The Titanic transcended beauty and historic beyond, providing a slice of her grandeur to all who embarked. She changed into, in her essence, a vessel of desires for the many who had set foot on her decks.

As passengers streamed onto the deliver, they carried their luggage and the desires and aspirations of a worldwide in the throes of transformation. The Titanic became no longer just a deliver putting sail; she have become a declaration of an technology that had released proper right into a quest to overcome the elements, an embodiment of the relentless spirit of innovation that characterised the early 20th century. Her departure become no longer only a voyage but a promise of improvement.

www.ingramcontent.com/pod-product-compliance
Lightning Source LLC
Chambersburg PA
CBHW071448080526
44587CB00014B/2029